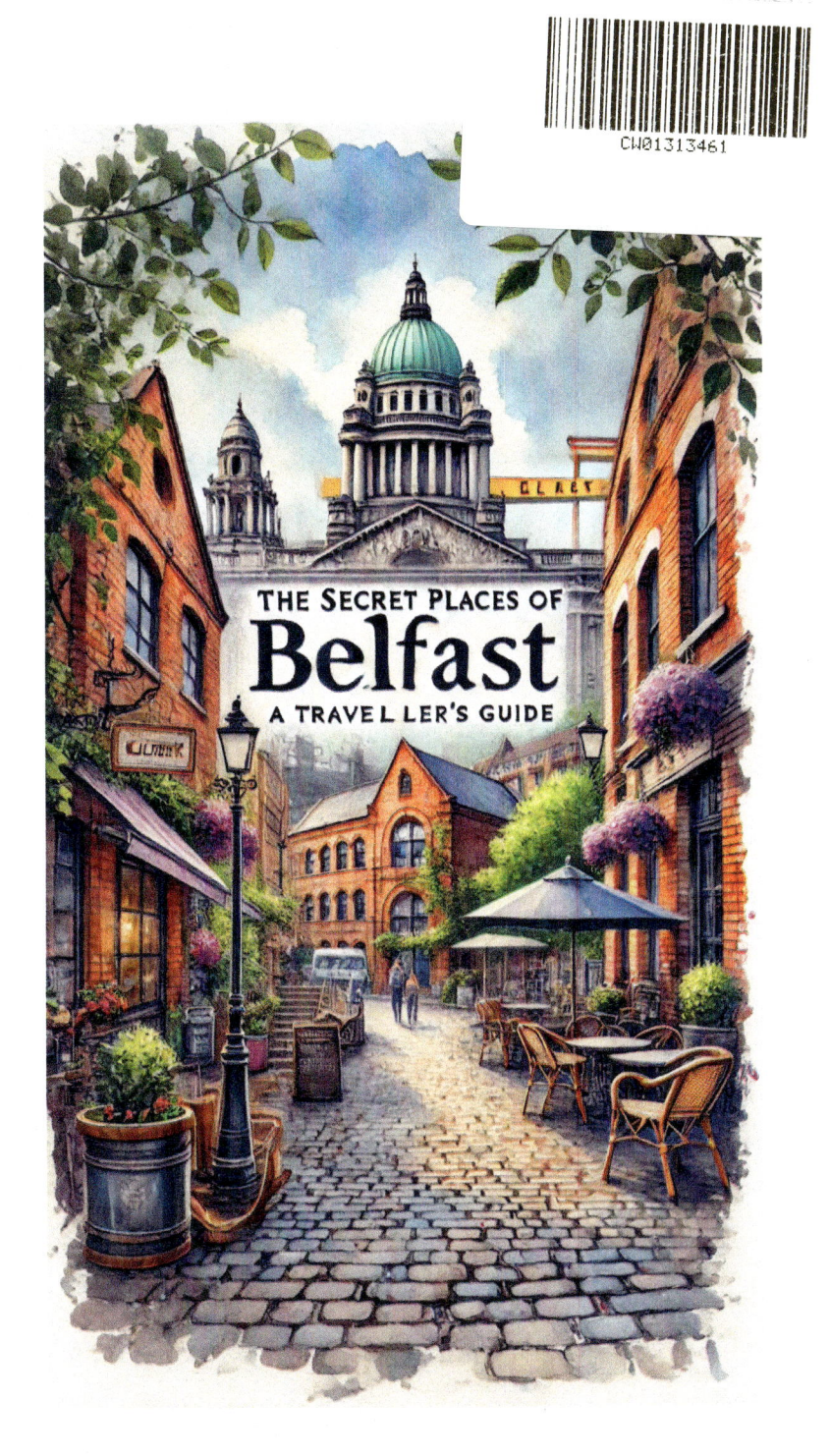

The Secret Places of
Belfast
A Traveller's Guide

Table of Contents

Introduction 4
    Welcome to Belfast 5
    How to Use This Guide... 5
    Brief History of Belfast 7

Chapter 1: 9
The Heart of the City 9
    City Hall... 10
    Victoria Square 13
    St. George's Market 17
    The Linen Quarter.. 21
    Cathedral Quarter 25
    Waterfront Hall 29
    Ulster Hall 33

Chapter 2: 37
Historical Landmarks 37
    Titanic Belfast 38
    SS Nomadic 41
    Harland & Wolff Cranes 45
    The Albert Clock.. 49
    Queen's University 53
    Belfast Castle 57

Chapter 3: 61
Natural Beauties 61
    Cave Hill... 62
    Botanic Gardens 66

Colin Glen Forest Park 71

Ormeau Park 76

The Lagan Towpath 82

Belfast Zoo 90

Chapter 4: 97

Hidden Gems 97

Secret Gardens and Courtyards 98

Murals and Street Art 102

Hidden Cafes and Bistros 107

Off-the-Beaten-Path Museums 112

Lesser-Known Pubs in Belfast 117

Chapter 5: Day Trips and Excursions 123

The Gobbins Cliff Path 124

Giant's Causeway 128

Carrickfergus Castle 132

Chapter 6: Practical Information 137

Accommodation 138

Transportation 144

Safety Tips 150

Local Customs and Etiquette 155

Useful Contacts 161

Appendices 167

Maps 167

Index 172

Acknowledgments 177

Introduction

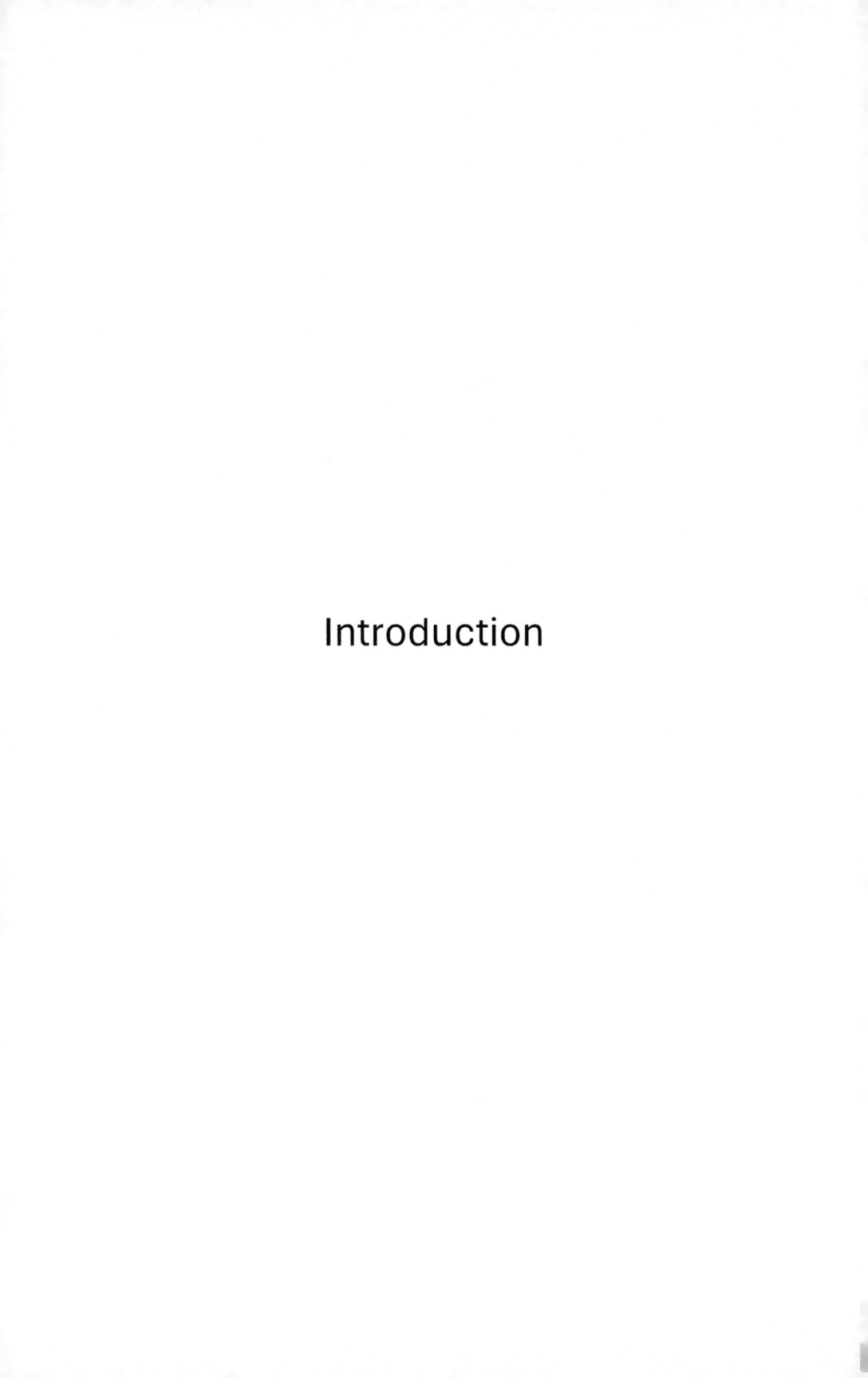

Welcome to Belfast

Nestled on the eastern coast of Northern Ireland, Belfast is a city brimming with rich history, vibrant culture, and hidden treasures waiting to be discovered. Known for its shipbuilding heritage and as the birthplace of the RMS Titanic, Belfast has transformed into a dynamic metropolis that seamlessly blends its storied past with a thriving contemporary scene. As you journey through its streets, you'll uncover a city that wears its history with pride while embracing a future filled with promise and creativity.

How to Use This Guide

This guide is designed to help you uncover the secret places of Belfast, offering a unique perspective on the city's well-known landmarks as well as its lesser-known gems. Each chapter is dedicated to different aspects of Belfast, from its bustling heart and historical landmarks to its natural beauties and hidden spots. Whether you're a first-time visitor or a seasoned traveller, this guide provides a comprehensive look at the city's diverse attractions.

Chapter 1: The Heart of the City introduces you to Belfast's vibrant city center, highlighting key locations that showcase its bustling urban life. You'll discover the grand City Hall, the shopping haven of Victoria Square, the lively St. George's Market, and the charming quarters that make up the core of Belfast's cultural and social scene.

Chapter 2: Historical Landmarks takes you on a journey through the city's rich past, with a focus on iconic sites that have shaped Belfast's identity. From the Titanic Belfast museum and the SS Nomadic to the towering Harland & Wolff cranes, you'll delve into the stories of Belfast's maritime heritage. Explore the historic Albert Clock, the prestigious Queen's University, and the stately Belfast Castle, each offering a glimpse into the city's storied past.

Chapter 3: Natural Beauties explores the serene and scenic landscapes that surround the city, offering a tranquil escape from urban life. Discover the breathtaking views from Cave Hill, the lush Botanic Gardens, and the peaceful Colin Glen Forest Park. Stroll along the Lagan Towpath, relax in Ormeau Park, or visit the diverse inhabitants of Belfast Zoo.

Chapter 4: Hidden Gems reveals the lesser-known, off-the-beaten-path spots that only the most curious explorers find. Uncover secret gardens and courtyards, marvel at vibrant murals and street art, and enjoy the cozy atmosphere of hidden cafes and bistros. This chapter also highlights off-the-beaten-path museums and lesser-known pubs where locals gather to unwind.

Chapter 5: Day Trips and Excursions suggests exciting adventures beyond the city limits, perfect for day trips and excursions. Embark on a thrilling walk along The Gobbins Cliff Path, marvel at the natural wonder of the Giant's Causeway, or explore the historic Carrickfergus Castle. Each destination offers a unique experience and a chance to see more of Northern Ireland's stunning landscapes and rich history.

Chapter 6: Practical Information provides essential tips on accommodation, transportation, safety, and local customs to ensure a smooth and enjoyable visit. Whether you're looking for a comfortable place to stay, navigating the city's transport system, or wanting to understand local etiquette, this chapter offers practical advice to help you make the most of your trip.

Brief History of Belfast

From its origins as a small settlement to its rise as a major industrial hub, Belfast's history is as captivating as it is complex. The city's name derives from the Irish "Béal Feirste," meaning "mouth of the sandbank ford," reflecting its early settlement near the River Lagan. The 19th century saw Belfast's growth explode during the Industrial Revolution, becoming renowned for its linen production, tobacco, ropemaking, and shipbuilding industries.

Belfast's most famous contribution to maritime history is undoubtedly the construction of the RMS Titanic, built at the Harland & Wolff shipyard. The city's history is also marked by the Troubles, a turbulent period of conflict from the late 1960s to the 1998 Good Friday Agreement, which has left an indelible mark on the city's identity. Despite these challenges, Belfast has emerged resilient, transforming into a city celebrated for its cultural vibrancy, innovation, and welcoming spirit.

Today, Belfast is a city reborn. Its historic buildings stand proudly alongside modern architecture, creating a skyline that tells a story of progress and heritage. The city is home to a thriving arts scene, with galleries, theatres, and music venues showcasing local and international talent. Festivals fill the calendar, celebrating everything from film and literature to food and music. The culinary scene has flourished, offering a mix of traditional fare and contemporary cuisine that reflects Belfast's diverse influences.

Get Ready to Explore

With this guide in hand, you're ready to uncover the secret places of Belfast. Whether you're wandering through historic streets, discovering hidden gardens, or sipping coffee in a tucked-away café, each page of this guide is a step towards experiencing the magic and mystery of this remarkable city. Prepare to be enchanted by Belfast's charm, captivated by its stories, and inspired by its resilience. Your journey through the secret places of Belfast begins here. Welcome to a city that is as intriguing as it is inviting.

Chapter 1:

The Heart of the City

City Hall

City Hall and Its History

Belfast City Hall stands as a magnificent centrepiece in the heart of the city, a symbol of Belfast's rich history and its journey through time. This iconic building, with its striking Baroque Revival architecture and imposing presence, is not only a functional space for city governance but also a cultural and historical landmark that tells the story of Belfast's evolution.

Architectural Grandeur

Completed in 1906, Belfast City Hall was built to celebrate Belfast's elevation to city status by Queen Victoria in 1888. The design, chosen through a competition, was the brainchild of Sir Alfred Brumwell Thomas, a renowned English architect. His vision brought to life a grand structure featuring Portland stone, copper-domed roofs, and intricate detailing that exudes opulence and authority. The central dome, which rises to a height of 53 meters, is particularly impressive, making the City Hall a prominent feature of Belfast's skyline.

Historical Significance

City Hall was constructed during a period of significant growth and prosperity for Belfast, driven largely by its flourishing linen and shipbuilding industries. This era saw the city transform into a major industrial hub, and the new City Hall was intended to reflect Belfast's newfound wealth and importance. The building's grandeur was a statement of civic pride and ambition, symbolizing the city's aspirations and achievements.

A Place of Governance and Celebration

Throughout its history, City Hall has been the epicentre of local government and public life in Belfast. It houses the council chamber where the Belfast City Council meets, along with the Lord Mayor's parlour and various offices for city officials. The building's public areas, including the rotunda and grand staircase, are adorned with beautiful stained glass windows, marble floors, and artworks that celebrate Belfast's heritage and notable figures.

City Hall is also a place of celebration and commemoration. Its grounds and gardens host numerous public events, from festivals and concerts to solemn remembrance ceremonies. The Titanic Memorial Garden, unveiled in 2012, honours the victims of the RMS Titanic, built in Belfast's shipyards. The grounds are a popular gathering spot for locals and tourists alike, offering a serene oasis amidst the bustling city.

Historical Moments

Over the years, Belfast City Hall has witnessed many significant events. During the tumultuous period of the Troubles, the building stood as a symbol of resilience amidst the conflict. In more recent times, it has been a site for important civic ceremonies, including the conferment of the Freedom of the City and celebrations marking major milestones in the city's history.

Visiting City Hall

Today, Belfast City Hall remains a must-visit attraction for anyone exploring the city. Guided tours are available, offering visitors a chance to delve into the building's history, architecture, and the role it plays in the life of the city. The tours provide a glimpse into the council chamber, the opulent reception rooms, and the impressive dome.

The visitor exhibition, located in the East Wing, is a modern addition that enhances the City Hall experience. It features interactive displays and exhibits that chronicle Belfast's story, from its early days to its rise as an industrial powerhouse and its ongoing transformation into a vibrant, modern city.

Summary

Belfast City Hall is more than just a seat of local government; it is a testament to the city's resilience, ambition, and rich cultural heritage. Its architectural splendor and historical significance make it a beacon of civic pride, embodying the spirit of Belfast and its people.

Victoria Square

Victoria Square stands as one of Belfast's premier shopping and leisure destinations, a modern architectural marvel that seamlessly blends retail, dining, and entertainment in the heart of the city. Opened in March 2008, this vibrant complex quickly became a landmark, drawing both locals and tourists with its unique design and extensive array of offerings.

Architectural Brilliance

The centrepiece of Victoria Square is its stunning glass dome, an architectural feat that rises above the complex, providing panoramic views of the city. Designed by the internationally renowned architects BDP (Building Design Partnership), the dome is not just a striking visual element but also a functional space. Visitors can take an elevator to the viewing platform, where they are treated to a 360-degree view of Belfast, including sights such as the Belfast City Hall, the Harland & Wolff cranes, and even the distant Cave Hill.

The overall design of Victoria Square is a blend of modern aesthetics and practical urban planning. The complex is spread across four levels, with a mix of covered and open-air spaces that create a dynamic shopping environment. The use of natural light, through extensive glazing and the open design, enhances the shopping experience, making it both pleasant and visually appealing.

A Shopper's Paradise

Victoria Square is home to over 70 shops, ranging from high-end fashion brands to popular high street retailers. Flagship stores like House of Fraser anchor the complex, offering a wide range of products from luxury fashion to home goods. Other notable retailers include Apple, H&M, and Topshop, ensuring that shoppers have access to the latest trends and technology.

In addition to fashion and retail stores, Victoria Square features specialty shops and boutiques that offer unique products, from bespoke jewelry to artisanal food items. This variety ensures that there is something for everyone, whether you are looking for a new outfit, a special gift, or just a leisurely day of window shopping.

Dining and Entertainment

Victoria Square is not just about shopping; it is also a hub for dining and entertainment. The complex boasts a diverse selection of restaurants, cafes, and bars, catering to a wide range of tastes and preferences.

From quick bites to gourmet meals, visitors can enjoy cuisines from around the world. Popular eateries include Yo! Sushi, Wagamama, and TGI Fridays, providing a mix of international flavours and local favourites.

For those looking to relax and unwind, the Odeon Cinema within Victoria Square offers a state-of-the-art movie-going experience. With multiple screens and comfortable seating, it is a great place to catch the latest blockbusters or enjoy a classic film. The cinema is a popular choice for both family outings and date nights, adding to the complex's appeal as an all-in-one destination.

Top tip: Visit the very top of Victoria square for beautiful scenes of Belfast!

Cultural and Community Events

Victoria Square is more than just a commercial center; it plays an active role in the community by hosting a variety of events throughout the year. From fashion shows and product launches to seasonal celebrations and charity fundraisers, the complex is a vibrant part of Belfast's social fabric. These events not only provide entertainment but also foster a sense of community, bringing people together in a shared space.

During holidays such as Christmas and Halloween, Victoria Square transforms with festive decorations, special performances, and activities that delight visitors of all ages. These celebrations add to the vibrant atmosphere, making each visit a unique experience.

Sustainable and Accessible

Victoria Square was designed with sustainability in mind. The building incorporates energy-efficient systems and materials, aiming to reduce its environmental impact. The complex also emphasizes accessibility, with features such as wide walkways, elevators, and ramps ensuring that it is welcoming to all visitors, including those with mobility challenges.

Summary of Victoria Square

Victoria Square is a testament to Belfast's ability to blend tradition with modernity. Its iconic glass dome and contemporary design set it apart as a landmark, while its diverse range of shops, dining options, and entertainment make it a must-visit destination. Whether you are a local resident or a tourist exploring Belfast, Victoria Square offers a vibrant and enjoyable experience, reflecting the dynamic spirit of the city.

St. George's Market

St. George's Market is one of Belfast's oldest attractions and one of the best markets in the UK and Ireland. This historic Victorian market, located on May Street, has been a staple of the city's community since its opening in 1890. Known for its vibrant atmosphere, diverse offerings, and rich heritage, St. George's Market is a beloved landmark that showcases the best of Belfast's local culture and produce.

Historical Significance

The origins of St. George's Market can be traced back to the 17th century when markets were held in various locations around Belfast. The current market building was constructed in three phases between 1890 and 1896, designed by the architect J.C. Bretland. It was built on the site of an earlier market that had become too small to accommodate the growing number of traders and customers. The new building featured a large, covered space with Victorian architectural elements, including ornate wrought iron columns and large arched windows that allowed natural light to flood the interior.

Over the years, the market has undergone several renovations and refurbishments to preserve its historical charm while enhancing its functionality. In 1997, a major restoration project was undertaken, resulting in the modern, vibrant market that exists today. This renovation helped to secure the market's place as a key attraction in Belfast, drawing locals and tourists alike.

Market Days and Offerings

St. George's Market operates three main market days, each offering a unique experience:

Friday Variety Market: This market day, held every Friday, features a wide range of stalls selling everything from fresh produce and seafood to antiques and vintage items. The variety market is a treasure trove for bargain hunters and those looking to explore an eclectic mix of goods. It also includes a selection of arts and crafts, adding to the diverse array of products available.

Saturday City Food and Craft Market: On Saturdays, the market transforms into a food lover's paradise, with an emphasis on local and artisanal produce. Stalls offer a delectable selection of fresh meats, cheeses, baked goods, and organic vegetables. In addition to food, the market boasts an impressive range of handmade crafts, jewelry, and artwork. Live music performances add to the lively atmosphere, making it a popular destination for both shopping and socializing.

Sunday Market: The Sunday market is a fusion of the best elements of the Friday and Saturday markets, with a focus on local crafts, food, and antiques. It has a relaxed and family-friendly vibe, attracting a diverse crowd looking to enjoy a leisurely market experience. The Sunday market also often features live entertainment, including traditional Irish music and dance, enhancing the cultural experience for visitors.

Activity: There is a stall dedicated to books from Belfast in St. Georges Market, can you find the stall with this book?

Community and Cultural Hub

St. George's Market is more than just a place to shop; it is a vibrant community hub that plays a significant role in Belfast's cultural life. The market provides a platform for local artisans, farmers, and small businesses to showcase their products, fostering a sense of community and supporting the local economy. It is a place where people come together, not only to buy and sell but also to connect and share stories.

> 'What's the Craic'?' — A Belfast phrase for how are you doing.

The market's lively atmosphere is enhanced by the regular live music performances, featuring local musicians and bands that create a festive ambiance. Special events and themed markets are held throughout the year, including seasonal markets for Christmas and Easter, as well as food festivals and craft fairs.

Architectural Charm

The architectural beauty of St. George's Market adds to its appeal. The building's Victorian design, with its wrought iron features and expansive glass windows, creates a charming and picturesque setting. Inside, the high ceilings and spacious layout provide a comfortable and airy environment for shoppers. The recent renovations have preserved these historical elements while incorporating modern amenities, ensuring that the market remains a functional and enjoyable space for all visitors.

St. George's Market is a testament to Belfast's rich history and vibrant community spirit. Its blend of traditional and contemporary offerings makes it a unique destination that caters to a wide range of interests. Whether you're a food enthusiast, an antique collector, or simply looking to experience the local culture, St. George's Market offers a welcoming and dynamic environment. As one of Belfast's most cherished landmarks, it continues to be a focal point of the city's social and cultural life, celebrating the best of what Belfast has to offer.

The Linen Quarter

The Linen Quarter is one of Belfast's most dynamic and historically rich districts. Named after the once-thriving linen industry that dominated the area in the 19th and early 20th centuries, the Linen Quarter has undergone a significant transformation in recent years. Today, it is a bustling urban hub known for its blend of historic architecture, modern amenities, and vibrant cultural scene.

Historical Background

Belfast's prominence as a linen manufacturing center dates back to the 18th century. By the mid-19th century, the city had earned the nickname "Linenopolis" due to its pivotal role in the global linen trade. The Linen Quarter was the heart of this industry, home to many of the city's linen mills, warehouses, and offices. These buildings, characterized by their red-brick facades and ornate detailing, still stand today, offering a glimpse into the area's industrious past.

The decline of the linen industry in the mid-20th century led to a period of stagnation for the district. However, in recent years, the Linen Quarter has experienced a renaissance, driven by a combination of urban regeneration initiatives and private investment. The district has been revitalized, preserving its historical charm while adapting to modern needs.

Architectural Heritage

One of the most striking features of the Linen Quarter is its architectural heritage. The area is dotted with beautifully restored Victorian and Edwardian buildings, many of which have been repurposed for contemporary use. Landmarks such as the Ormeau Baths, once a public bathhouse and now a tech hub, exemplify this blend of old and new.

Walking through the Linen Quarter, visitors can admire the intricate brickwork, grand facades, and historic detailing that characterize the district's architecture. Many buildings have been converted into offices, hotels, restaurants, and cultural venues, ensuring that the area's heritage is preserved and appreciated.

Modern Transformation

The Linen Quarter's transformation into a vibrant urban district is marked by a surge in new developments and amenities. The area is now home to a mix of commercial, residential, and leisure facilities, making it a lively destination for both locals and visitors.

Hotels like the luxurious Grand Central Hotel and the stylish Ten Square Hotel offer upscale accommodation options, while a range of dining establishments cater to diverse tastes. From trendy cafes and gastropubs to fine dining restaurants, the Linen Quarter boasts a culinary scene that reflects Belfast's growing reputation as a foodie destination.

The district is also a burgeoning business hub, attracting tech companies, creative industries, and professional services. Co-working spaces and office buildings provide flexible work environments, contributing to the area's dynamic and entrepreneurial spirit.

Cultural and Social Hub

The Linen Quarter is not just about business and commerce; it is also a cultural and social hub. The district hosts a variety of events throughout the year, from music festivals and street performances to art exhibitions and food markets. These events draw people from across the city and beyond, creating a vibrant community atmosphere.

One of the key cultural venues in the Linen Quarter is the Ulster Hall, a historic concert hall that has been a cornerstone of Belfast's cultural life since 1862. The hall hosts a diverse program of concerts, theatre performances, and community events, maintaining its status as a beloved institution in the city.

Green spaces and public art installations add to the district's appeal. Linenhall Street and Bedford Street are particularly noted for their green initiatives, with tree-lined streets, pocket parks, and pedestrian-friendly areas enhancing the urban environment.

Connectivity and Accessibility

The Linen Quarter's central location makes it highly accessible and well-connected. It is situated adjacent to the city center, with easy access to major transport links including the Belfast Central Railway Station and the Europa Bus Centre. This connectivity ensures that the district is a convenient destination for both business and leisure travellers.

Conclusion

The Linen Quarter stands as a testament to Belfast's ability to honor its past while embracing the future. Its blend of historic charm and modern vibrancy makes it a unique and compelling district within the city. Whether you're exploring its architectural heritage, enjoying its culinary delights, or participating in its cultural events, the Linen Quarter offers a rich and diverse experience that captures the essence of Belfast's ongoing transformation.

Cathedral Quarter

The Cathedral Quarter is one of Belfast's most vibrant and culturally rich districts. Named after St. Anne's Cathedral, also known as Belfast Cathedral, this area has transformed from an industrial and commercial hub into the beating heart of the city's arts and entertainment scene. With its cobblestone streets, historic buildings, and eclectic mix of venues, the Cathedral Quarter offers a unique blend of history, culture, and modern vibrancy.

Historical Background

The Cathedral Quarter's history dates back to the 17th century, when Belfast was little more than a small settlement. The area developed rapidly during the Industrial Revolution, becoming a center for trade and commerce. Many of the buildings that stand today were originally warehouses, factories, and merchants' offices, reflecting the area's industrious past.

In recent decades, the Cathedral Quarter has undergone significant regeneration. Efforts to preserve its historical character while fostering a creative and cultural environment have transformed the district into one of Belfast's most dynamic areas. The juxtaposition of old and new is evident throughout the Quarter, with contemporary art installations and trendy bars nestled alongside historic architecture.

St. Anne's Cathedral

At the heart of the Cathedral Quarter is St. Anne's Cathedral, a stunning example of Romanesque architecture. Construction began in 1899, and the cathedral has since become an iconic landmark. It features beautiful stained-glass windows, intricate mosaics, and a prominent spire added in 2007 known as the Spire of Hope. The cathedral is not only a place of worship but also a cultural venue, hosting concerts, exhibitions, and community events.

Arts and Culture

The Cathedral Quarter is renowned for its thriving arts scene. The district is home to a variety of galleries, theatres, and performance spaces that cater to diverse artistic tastes. The MAC (Metropolitan Arts Centre) is a standout venue, offering a dynamic program of visual art, theatre, dance, and music. With its modern design and versatile spaces, the MAC is a cultural cornerstone in the district.

Street art is another prominent feature of the Cathedral Quarter. Murals and installations by local and international artists adorn the walls, adding color and creativity to the urban landscape. These works of art are not only visually striking but also reflect the area's commitment to fostering a vibrant artistic community.

Dining and Nightlife

The Cathedral Quarter boasts a bustling dining and nightlife scene, with a wide range of pubs, restaurants, and cafes. The Duke of York, a historic pub with a charming courtyard, is a favorite among locals and visitors alike. Its cozy atmosphere, traditional decor, and extensive whiskey selection make it a must-visit spot.

For those seeking culinary delights, the district offers an array of options. From fine dining establishments like The Muddlers Club, which offers contemporary cuisine in an intimate setting, to casual eateries and food markets, there is something to satisfy every palate. Many venues also feature live music, creating a lively and entertaining dining experience.

Festivals and Events

The Cathedral Quarter is a hub for festivals and events, attracting crowds from near and far. The annual Cathedral Quarter Arts Festival is a highlight, showcasing a diverse lineup of music, theater, literature, and visual arts. This ten-day event transforms the district into a cultural playground, with performances and exhibitions taking place in venues large and small.

Other notable events include the Belfast Film Festival and Culture Night Belfast, which celebrate the city's creative spirit through film screenings, street performances, and interactive art installations. These festivals not only provide entertainment but also foster a sense of community and celebrate Belfast's cultural diversity.

Historic Sites and Landmarks

In addition to St. Anne's Cathedral, the Cathedral Quarter is home to several historic sites and landmarks. The Northern Whig, a former newspaper office turned stylish bar, retains much of its original grandeur with its neoclassical facade and ornate interior. The Custom House, an imposing Victorian building, is another architectural gem that has been repurposed for modern use.

Walking through the district, visitors can also explore Writer's Square, a public space dedicated to Northern Irish writers and poets. Quotes and literary works are inscribed on the pavement, offering inspiration and a sense of connection to the region's rich literary heritage.

Conclusion

The Cathedral Quarter is a testament to Belfast's ability to embrace its history while fostering a vibrant, contemporary cultural scene. Its blend of historic charm, artistic innovation, and lively social atmosphere make it a unique and compelling district within the city. Whether you're exploring its architectural treasures, enjoying its artistic offerings, or simply soaking in the atmosphere at a local pub, the Cathedral Quarter offers a rich and diverse experience that captures the essence of Belfast's creative spirit.

Waterfront Hall

Waterfront Hall is one of Belfast's premier venues for concerts, conferences, and events, offering a stunning combination of modern architecture, state-of-the-art facilities, and a prime location on the banks of the River Lagan. Since its opening in 1997, Waterfront Hall has become an iconic symbol of Belfast's cultural and economic revitalization, attracting visitors from around the world for a wide range of performances and events.

Architectural Marvel

Designed by the architecture firm Robinson McIlwaine, Waterfront Hall is a striking example of contemporary design. The building's exterior features a curved glass facade that offers panoramic views of the River Lagan and the cityscape beyond. This use of glass not only creates a sense of openness and transparency but also allows natural light to flood the interior spaces, enhancing the building's aesthetic appeal.

The centerpiece of Waterfront Hall is its main auditorium, which boasts excellent acoustics and seating for up to 2,241 people. The auditorium's flexible design allows it to accommodate a variety of events, from large-scale concerts and theatrical performances to conferences and community gatherings. The hall also includes a smaller studio space, which is ideal for more intimate events and performances.

A Hub for Entertainment

Waterfront Hall is renowned for its diverse program of events, which includes everything from classical music and opera to pop concerts, comedy shows, and theatrical productions. Over the years, it has hosted performances by world-famous artists and orchestras, as well as local talent, making it a central part of Belfast's cultural landscape.

The venue is also a key player in Belfast's festival scene, often serving as a primary location for events such as the Belfast International Arts Festival, the Belfast Film Festival, and the Cathedral Quarter Arts Festival. These events bring together artists and audiences from across the globe, fostering a vibrant cultural exchange and enhancing the city's reputation as a cultural capital.

Conference and Event Space

In addition to its role as an entertainment venue, Waterfront Hall is a major center for conferences and corporate events. The building's versatile spaces can accommodate events of all sizes, from small meetings and workshops to large international conferences. The main auditorium, studio space, and several meeting rooms are equipped with the latest audiovisual technology, ensuring that events run smoothly and efficiently.

Waterfront Hall's prime location in the heart of Belfast's business district makes it a convenient choice for corporate events. Its proximity to hotels, restaurants, and transportation links adds to its appeal, providing attendees with easy access to all the amenities they need during their stay.

Community Engagement

Waterfront Hall is deeply committed to community engagement and education. The venue hosts a variety of outreach programs and workshops aimed at inspiring and nurturing local talent. These initiatives include music and drama workshops for young people, educational tours, and collaborations with schools and community groups.

The hall's commitment to accessibility ensures that everyone can enjoy its offerings. Facilities such as wheelchair-accessible seating, hearing induction loops, and assistance for visually impaired visitors are in place to make the venue inclusive for all members of the community.

Sustainability and Innovation

Waterfront Hall is also dedicated to sustainability and environmental responsibility. The building's design incorporates energy-efficient systems and sustainable materials, minimizing its environmental impact. Initiatives such as recycling programs, energy conservation measures, and sustainable sourcing practices are part of the venue's ongoing efforts to promote environmental stewardship.

Conclusion

Waterfront Hall stands as a testament to Belfast's resurgence as a vibrant, forward-thinking city. Its blend of cutting-edge architecture, world-class facilities, and diverse programming makes it a cornerstone of the city's cultural and economic life. Whether attending a concert, participating in a conference, or simply enjoying the views of the River Lagan, visitors to Waterfront Hall experience the best of what Belfast has to offer.

The hall's commitment to excellence, community engagement, and sustainability ensures that it will continue to be a beloved and essential part of Belfast's landscape for years to come. Whether you're a local resident or a visitor to the city, a trip to Waterfront Hall promises a memorable experience that captures the spirit of Belfast's cultural renaissance.

Ulster Hall

Ulster Hall is one of Belfast's most cherished cultural landmarks, renowned for its rich history, architectural beauty, and role as a premier venue for music and events. Opened in 1862, Ulster Hall has hosted a wide array of performances and gatherings, making it a central part of Belfast's social and cultural fabric for over 150 years.

Historical Background

Ulster Hall was designed by the celebrated architect William J. Barre, known for his distinctive and ornate style. The hall was constructed to serve as a multi-purpose venue for concerts, public meetings, and exhibitions. Its opening was marked by a grand concert featuring the renowned pianist and composer William Sterndale Bennett.

Throughout its long history, Ulster Hall has witnessed many significant events. It has served as a platform for political speeches, including addresses by British Prime Ministers and Irish leaders. The hall was also a focal point for social and charitable events, playing a vital role in the community.

Architectural Splendor

The architecture of Ulster Hall is a fine example of Victorian design, characterized by its elegant facade and intricate interior detailing. The building's exterior features a classical design with a portico supported by

Corinthian columns, creating a grand and imposing entrance.

Inside, the hall is equally impressive. The main auditorium, known as the Mulholland Grand Organ Hall, is named after the magnificent pipe organ donated by local businessman Andrew Mulholland. The organ, built by the renowned firm William Hill & Son, is one of the finest examples of its kind and a focal point of the hall's interior.

The auditorium is adorned with ornate plasterwork, a beautiful ceiling rose, and elegant balconies that enhance its acoustic properties. The combination of these elements creates an intimate yet grand atmosphere, making it a beloved venue for both performers and audiences.

A Venue for Music and the Arts

Ulster Hall has a long-standing reputation as a premier venue for music and the arts. It has hosted performances by some of the world's most famous musicians and bands, spanning genres from classical and jazz to rock and pop. Notable performers who have graced its stage include Led Zeppelin, Rory Gallagher, and the Rolling Stones, cementing its status as an iconic music venue.

The hall is also home to the Ulster Orchestra, Northern Ireland's professional symphony orchestra. The orchestra's regular concerts at Ulster Hall are a highlight of Belfast's cultural calendar, attracting music lovers from near and far.

In addition to music, Ulster Hall hosts a variety of other events, including theatrical performances, comedy shows, literary readings, and public lectures. Its versatile spaces can accommodate different types of events, making it a vital part of Belfast's cultural scene.

Community and Educational Engagement

Ulster Hall is deeply committed to engaging with the local community and promoting arts education. The venue offers a range of outreach programs and workshops designed to inspire and nurture young talent. These initiatives include music education programs, interactive tours, and collaborations with schools and community groups.

The hall's accessible facilities ensure that everyone can enjoy its events. Features such as wheelchair-accessible seating, hearing induction loops, and assistance for visually impaired visitors are in place to make the venue welcoming and inclusive for all.

Preservation and Restoration

Over the years, Ulster Hall has undergone several renovations to preserve its historical features and enhance its facilities. A major refurbishment project in the early 2000s ensured that the hall remained fit for contemporary use while retaining its Victorian charm. The restoration work included upgrades to the building's infrastructure, improvements to the acoustics, and the conservation of its historic elements.

Conclusion

Ulster Hall stands as a testament to Belfast's rich cultural heritage and enduring love for the arts. Its blend of historical significance, architectural beauty, and vibrant programming makes it a cornerstone of the city's cultural life. Whether attending a concert, participating in a community event, or simply admiring its grandeur, visitors to Ulster Hall experience a piece of Belfast's history and its dynamic cultural scene.

As it continues to host a diverse array of performances and events, Ulster Hall remains a vital and beloved venue in Belfast, celebrating the past while embracing the future. Its legacy as a cultural icon ensures that it will continue to inspire and entertain for generations to come.

Chapter 2:

Historical Landmarks

Titanic Belfast

Titanic Belfast is one of the most iconic and visited attractions in Northern Ireland, dedicated to the history of the RMS Titanic and the city's maritime heritage. Opened in 2012, this striking building stands on the site of the former Harland & Wolff shipyard in the Titanic Quarter, where the infamous ship was designed and built. The museum offers an immersive and educational experience, drawing visitors from around the world to explore the legacy of the Titanic and Belfast's shipbuilding past.

Architectural Marvel

The architecture of Titanic Belfast is as impressive as the story it tells. Designed by Eric Kuhne and Associates, the building's angular, silver-clad exterior is reminiscent of the hulls of ships, with its star-shaped footprint symbolizing the White Star Line. Standing at 126 feet high, the same height as the Titanic's hull, the building makes a bold statement against the backdrop of the Titanic Quarter.

The interior is equally remarkable, featuring a series of galleries and exhibition spaces that guide visitors through the Titanic's journey from conception to its tragic end. The design incorporates cutting-edge technology and innovative displays to create an engaging and educational experience.

The Titanic Experience

The Titanic Experience is the main attraction of Titanic Belfast, offering nine interactive galleries that take visitors on a journey through the history of the Titanic. The experience begins with Boomtown Belfast, a gallery that sets the stage by showcasing Belfast's industrial prowess in the early 20th century, highlighting the city's role as a leading shipbuilding center.

The second gallery, The Arrol Gantry and Shipyard Ride, immerses visitors in the construction of the Titanic. Using a combination of special effects and a thrilling ride, it brings the scale and ambition of the shipyard to life. Visitors can explore a detailed replica of the Titanic's hull and witness the ship's launch in 1911.

The Fit-Out gallery provides a glimpse into the luxurious interiors of the Titanic, featuring recreations of the ship's grand staircase, cabins, and dining rooms. This gallery highlights the opulence and craftsmanship that went into creating what was then the world's most luxurious ocean liner.

The Maiden Voyage gallery chronicles the Titanic's ill-fated journey across the Atlantic, complete with interactive maps and personal stories of passengers and crew. Visitors can walk along a glass floor that simulates the ocean, adding a dramatic touch to the experience.

The Sinking and Aftermath galleries take a poignant turn, detailing the events of April 14-15, 1912, when the Titanic struck an iceberg and sank. These galleries use immersive displays to convey the tragedy, including audio recordings of survivors' testimonies and visuals of the lifeboats.

Finally, the Myths & Legends and Titanic Beneath galleries explore the aftermath of the disaster and the enduring legacy of the Titanic. Visitors can learn about the numerous myths surrounding the ship, as well as the scientific efforts to locate and explore the wreckage on the ocean floor.

Maritime and Industrial Heritage

In addition to the Titanic Experience, Titanic Belfast celebrates Belfast's broader maritime and industrial heritage. The museum's location in the Titanic Quarter, once the bustling heart of the city's shipbuilding industry, adds historical authenticity to the experience. Visitors can explore the original Harland & Wolff drawing offices, where the Titanic and her sister ships were designed, as well as the slipways where the Titanic was launched.

The museum also offers insights into other notable ships built in Belfast, such as the SS Nomadic, the last remaining White Star Line vessel, which served as a tender to the Titanic and is now preserved as a museum ship nearby.

Events and Educational Programs

Titanic Belfast is not just a museum but also a dynamic cultural venue that hosts a variety of events and educational programs. These include special exhibitions, lectures, film screenings, and workshops aimed at both adults and children. The museum's educational outreach programs engage schools and community groups, fostering a deeper understanding of maritime history and engineering.

Conclusion

Titanic Belfast stands as a testament to the city's shipbuilding legacy and the enduring fascination with the story of the Titanic. Its innovative design, comprehensive exhibits, and immersive experiences make it a must-visit destination for anyone interested in history, maritime heritage, or the tragic tale of the Titanic. As a symbol of Belfast's industrial past and its ongoing cultural renaissance, Titanic Belfast continues to attract and inspire visitors from around the globe. Whether you're a history enthusiast, a curious traveler, or someone seeking to understand the human stories behind the legend, Titanic Belfast offers a poignant and memorable journey through time.

SS Nomadic

The SS Nomadic is an integral part of Belfast's rich maritime heritage and offers a unique connection to the story of the RMS Titanic. Built in 1911, the Nomadic served as a tender to the Titanic and her sister ship, the RMS Olympic, ferrying passengers, baggage, and supplies from the port of Cherbourg, France, to the larger ocean liners. Today, the SS Nomadic is preserved as a museum ship in Belfast's Titanic

Quarter, providing visitors with a tangible link to the Golden Age of ocean travel.

Historical Background

The SS Nomadic was commissioned by the White Star Line and constructed at the Harland & Wolff shipyard in Belfast, the same shipyard that built the Titanic. Designed by Thomas Andrews, the chief naval architect for Harland & Wolff, the Nomadic was launched on April 25, 1911, just a few months before the Titanic.

Nomadic's primary role was to transport first and second-class passengers from the port of Cherbourg to the waiting ocean liners anchored offshore. This was necessary because Cherbourg's harbor was too shallow to accommodate the larger ships. The Nomadic's robust design and luxurious interiors made it a fitting precursor to boarding the opulent Titanic.

Service Life

The SS Nomadic began its service career in June 1911, and its first major task was ferrying passengers to the RMS Olympic. When the Titanic set sail on its maiden voyage in April 1912, the Nomadic played a crucial role in boarding prominent passengers in Cherbourg, including John Jacob Astor IV, Molly Brown, and Benjamin Guggenheim.

After the Titanic disaster, the Nomadic continued to serve the White Star Line, eventually being acquired by other shipping companies and repurposed for various roles, including a troopship during both World Wars and a floating restaurant on the River Seine in Paris. Throughout its diverse service life, the Nomadic remained remarkably well-preserved.

Preservation and Restoration

In 2006, after decades of varied use and some neglect, the SS Nomadic was purchased by the Department for Social Development in Northern Ireland, with the aim of restoring it as part of Belfast's maritime heritage. The ship was returned to Belfast in 2006, where extensive restoration work began to return it to its former glory.

The restoration project focused on preserving the ship's historical integrity while making it safe and accessible for visitors. This involved refurbishing the hull, superstructure, and interiors to reflect the ship's original 1911 condition as accurately as possible. The project was completed with great care, ensuring that visitors could experience the Nomadic as it would have appeared to passengers over a century ago.

Visitor Experience

Today, the SS Nomadic is berthed at Hamilton Dock, adjacent to the Titanic Belfast museum. As the last remaining White Star Line vessel, the Nomadic offers a unique and authentic glimpse into the past. Visitors can explore the ship's decks, passenger areas, and crew quarters, all meticulously restored to their early 20th-century appearance.

The visitor experience is enhanced by interactive exhibits and knowledgeable guides who provide detailed insights into the ship's history, its connection to the Titanic, and its varied service life. The exhibits include artifacts, photographs, and personal stories from the ship's past, creating a vivid picture of what life was like aboard this historic vessel.

The Nomadic's significance is further underscored by its connection to many of the Titanic's notable passengers. Walking the decks of the Nomadic, visitors can imagine the anticipation and excitement of those who were ferried to the Titanic on its fateful maiden voyage.

Educational and Cultural Importance

The SS Nomadic is not just a museum ship; it also serves as an important educational resource. Schools and educational groups frequently visit the ship to learn about maritime history, engineering, and the socio-economic context of the early 20th century. The Nomadic's preservation and presentation offer valuable lessons in heritage conservation and the importance of preserving historical artifacts for future generations.

In addition to its educational role, the Nomadic hosts a variety of cultural and community events. These events range from historical reenactments and maritime festivals to private functions and corporate events, making the ship a versatile venue that continues to serve the community.

Conclusion

The SS Nomadic is a cherished part of Belfast's maritime legacy, offering a direct link to the story of the Titanic and the broader history of the White Star Line. Its preservation as a museum ship allows visitors to step back in time and experience a piece of living history. As part of the Titanic Quarter, the Nomadic complements the Titanic Belfast museum, enriching the narrative of Belfast's shipbuilding heritage and the Golden Age of ocean liners. Whether you're a history enthusiast, a maritime aficionado, or simply curious about the past, a visit to the SS Nomadic promises a fascinating and memorable journey into history.

Harland & Wolff Cranes

The Harland & Wolff cranes, Samson and Goliath, are among the most iconic landmarks in Belfast, symbolizing the city's rich shipbuilding heritage. These twin gantry cranes dominate the skyline of the Titanic Quarter, standing as proud reminders of the industrial prowess that once made Belfast one of the leading shipbuilding centers in the world. Their towering presence is a testament to the engineering marvels that were produced at the Harland & Wolff shipyard, including the RMS Titanic.

Historical Background

Harland & Wolff, founded in 1861 by Edward James Harland and Gustav Wilhelm Wolff, quickly became one of the most important shipyards globally. The company was renowned for constructing some of the largest and most famous ships of the early 20th century, including the RMS Titanic, RMS Olympic, and RMS Britannic, the trio known as the Olympic-class ocean liners.

The shipyard's ability to handle such monumental projects was greatly enhanced by the addition of two massive gantry cranes in the late 20th century. These cranes were named Samson and Goliath, fittingly named after the biblical figures known for their immense strength.

Construction and Specifications

Goliath, the older of the two cranes, was constructed in 1969. It stands at 96 meters (315 feet) tall with a span of 140 meters (459 feet). Samson, built in 1974, is slightly taller at 106 meters (348 feet) with a similar span. Both cranes have a lifting capacity of 840 tonnes, making them capable of handling the massive components of ships and offshore structures.

The construction of these cranes was a significant engineering feat. They were designed by the German engineering firm Krupp and built on-site, using advanced techniques to ensure they could support the heavy lifting required by the shipyard. The cranes' towering structures are made from steel, with a distinctive yellow paint that makes them visible from miles away.

Symbolism and Legacy

Samson and Goliath are not just functional pieces of equipment; they are symbols of Belfast's industrial heritage and the city's role in maritime history. During their peak operational years, the cranes played a crucial role in the construction of numerous ships and offshore platforms. They facilitated the assembly of large ship sections, heavy machinery, and complex structures, contributing to Harland & Wolff's reputation for quality and innovation.

Although the shipyard's activity has decreased significantly since its heyday, the cranes remain a potent symbol of Belfast's industrial legacy. They are a physical reminder of the thousands of skilled workers who contributed to the shipyard's success and the city's economic development.

Modern Significance and Preservation

Today, the Harland & Wolff cranes are no longer in regular use for shipbuilding but have been preserved as important historical and cultural landmarks. They are part of the Titanic Quarter, a major redevelopment area that celebrates Belfast's maritime heritage while promoting modern urban development.

The cranes are protected structures, recognized for their historical significance and iconic status. Efforts have been made to maintain them in good condition, ensuring that they continue to stand as proud symbols of Belfast's past. They attract tourists from around the world, many of whom visit the nearby Titanic Belfast museum and other historical sites in the Titanic Quarter.

Visitor Experience

Visiting the Harland & Wolff cranes offers a unique insight into Belfast's industrial history. While the cranes themselves are not accessible to the public, their imposing presence can be appreciated from various vantage points around the Titanic Quarter. Guided tours of the area often include detailed explanations of the cranes' history and their role in shipbuilding, providing context and enhancing the visitor experience.

Photographers and history enthusiasts find the cranes particularly captivating, as they provide a striking contrast between Belfast's industrial past and its modern transformation. The cranes are frequently featured in media and literature about the city, highlighting their enduring significance.

Conclusion

The Harland & Wolff cranes, Samson and Goliath, are towering symbols of Belfast's shipbuilding heritage and industrial strength. They stand as enduring reminders of the city's pivotal role in maritime history and the remarkable engineering achievements of the Harland & Wolff shipyard. While their practical use has diminished, their preservation as cultural landmarks ensures that they continue to inspire and educate future generations about Belfast's rich industrial legacy. Whether you're a history buff, an engineering enthusiast, or simply a visitor to Belfast, the sight of Samson and Goliath is a powerful testament to the city's storied past and its ongoing journey of transformation and renewal.

The Albert Clock

The Albert Clock is one of Belfast's most distinctive landmarks, often compared to London's Big Ben for its prominent presence and historical significance. Located at Queen's Square in the city center, this leaning clock tower is not only a functional timepiece but also a beloved symbol of Belfast's Victorian heritage and architectural charm.

Historical Background

The Albert Clock was erected in memory of Prince Albert, the consort of Queen Victoria, who passed away in 1861. The citizens of Belfast, wishing to honor the Prince's contributions and memory, decided to build a clock tower as a public monument.

The foundation stone was laid in 1865, and the tower was completed in 1869.

The tower was designed by William J. Barre, a renowned architect known for his work on other notable buildings in Belfast, including the Ulster Hall. The design of the Albert Clock reflects the Victorian Gothic style, characterized by intricate detailing, pointed arches, and a sense of verticality.

Architectural Features

Standing at 113 feet (34.5 meters) tall, the Albert Clock is constructed from sandstone, giving it a warm, golden appearance. The tower is adorned with decorative carvings, including floral motifs, heraldic symbols, and a statue of Prince Albert himself, which is positioned above the main entrance.

One of the most striking features of the Albert Clock is its clock face. Each of the four sides of the tower has a large clock face, allowing the time to be viewed from various directions. The clock mechanism was crafted by Francis Moore of High Street, Belfast, ensuring accuracy and reliability.

The base of the tower is designed to resemble the stern of a ship, a nod to Belfast's maritime heritage. This unique feature includes a lion and a unicorn, symbolizing the British monarchy, flanking a shield that bears the arms of Belfast.

The Leaning Tower of Belfast

Over the years, the Albert Clock has developed a noticeable tilt, earning it the nickname "The Leaning Tower of Belfast." This tilt is primarily due to the fact that the tower was built on land reclaimed from the River Farset, which flows underneath Queen's Square. The soft, marshy ground has caused the foundation to settle unevenly, leading to the tower's characteristic lean.

Despite the tilt, the Albert Clock remains structurally sound. In the early 2000s, a major restoration project was undertaken to clean and stabilize the tower, ensuring its preservation for future generations. The project included repairs to the clock mechanism, the stonework, and the foundation to prevent further leaning.

Cultural and Social Significance

The Albert Clock is more than just an architectural landmark; it is a symbol of Belfast's resilience and historical continuity. Over the years, it has witnessed the city's growth, changes, and challenges. The clock tower has become a popular meeting point for locals and a must-see attraction for tourists.

Throughout its history, the Albert Clock has been a focal point for public events and celebrations. It has also been referenced in literature, music, and art, cementing its place in Belfast's cultural landscape. The surrounding area, Queen's Square, is a bustling part of the city, home to shops, restaurants, and historic buildings, making the clock tower a central feature of the urban environment.

Visiting the Albert Clock

Today, the Albert Clock remains one of Belfast's top attractions. Visitors can admire the intricate details of its Gothic architecture, learn about its history through informational plaques, and appreciate the unique lean that has made it famous. The clock tower is particularly striking when illuminated at night, providing a picturesque view against the city skyline.

The Albert Clock is also conveniently located near other key attractions in Belfast, including the Custom House, the Big Fish sculpture, and the Cathedral Quarter, making it easy to include in a walking tour of the city. Its central location ensures that it is accessible and visible from various parts of the city center.

Conclusion

The Albert Clock stands as a testament to Belfast's Victorian heritage, architectural beauty, and historical resilience. Its combination of functional design, decorative artistry, and unique tilt make it a distinctive and beloved landmark in the heart of the city. Whether you are a history enthusiast, an architecture lover, or a casual visitor, the Albert Clock offers a fascinating glimpse into Belfast's past and continues to be a proud symbol of the city's enduring spirit.

Queen's University

Queen's University Belfast is one of the leading educational institutions in the United Kingdom, known for its rich history, distinguished academic programs, and stunning campus. Located in the heart of Belfast, the university has been a cornerstone of education, research, and cultural life in Northern Ireland since its founding in 1845.

Historical Background

Queen's University was established as one of three Queen's Colleges in Ireland, alongside those in Cork and Galway. It was part of a broader effort to provide higher education in Ireland during the reign of Queen Victoria, and it officially opened its doors in 1849. The institution was originally known as Queen's College, Belfast, and became a full university in 1908 when it received its Royal Charter.

The founding of Queen's University was driven by the need for a non-denominational institution that could provide high-quality education to a broad segment of society. Over the years, the university has grown and evolved, expanding its academic offerings and research capabilities to become a globally recognized center of excellence.

Architectural Highlights

The main campus of Queen's University is renowned for its architectural beauty, blending historic and modern buildings in a picturesque setting. The centerpiece is the iconic Lanyon Building, designed by Sir Charles Lanyon in the Gothic Revival style. Completed in 1849, the Lanyon Building features a striking facade with red brick, sandstone detailing, and ornate windows, making it one of the most photographed landmarks in Belfast.

Other notable buildings on campus include the Ashby Building, which houses the School of Engineering, and the McClay Library, a state-of-the-art facility that combines traditional library services with cutting-edge technology and design. The library, named after local philanthropist Sir Allen McClay, offers an inspiring environment for study and research.

The university's campus is also home to the Naughton Gallery, which hosts contemporary art exhibitions, and the Queen's Film Theatre, an independent cinema that showcases a diverse range of films, including independent, international, and classic cinema.

Academic Excellence

Queen's University is known for its strong emphasis on research and academic excellence. It offers a wide range of undergraduate and postgraduate programs across various fields, including arts and humanities, science and engineering, social sciences, and medicine. The university's research centers and institutes are at the forefront of innovation, making significant contributions to global knowledge and societal development.

Notable among its research institutions is the Institute of Electronics, Communications and Information Technology (ECIT), which is renowned for its work in cyber security, wireless communications, and data science. The Centre for Cancer Research and Cell Biology (CCRCB) is another leading research facility, focusing on pioneering cancer treatments and improving patient outcomes.

Queen's University is a member of the prestigious Russell Group, which represents 24 leading public research universities in the UK. This membership reflects the university's commitment to maintaining high standards in research, teaching, and learning.

Student Life

Student life at Queen's University is vibrant and diverse, with a wide range of extracurricular activities, clubs, and societies. The Queen's University Students' Union (QUBSU) provides support and services to students, as well as organizing events and activities that enhance the university experience. From academic societies and cultural groups to sports clubs and volunteer organizations, there are ample opportunities for students to engage, learn, and socialize.

The campus is located in a lively part of Belfast, close to Botanic Gardens, the Ulster Museum, and a variety of cafes, restaurants, and shops. This prime location allows students to enjoy the cultural and social amenities of the city while pursuing their studies.

Community Engagement and Impact

Queen's University is deeply committed to community engagement and social responsibility. The university works closely with local, national, and international partners to address societal challenges and contribute to economic development. Initiatives such as the Social Charter and the Queen's Communities and Place program demonstrate the university's dedication to making a positive impact beyond the campus.

The university also plays a significant role in promoting peace and reconciliation in Northern Ireland, supporting initiatives that foster understanding and cooperation among diverse communities.

Conclusion

Queen's University Belfast stands as a beacon of academic excellence, historical significance, and cultural vibrancy. Its beautiful campus, distinguished faculty, and commitment to research and community engagement make it a leading institution of higher learning. Whether you are a student, researcher, or visitor, Queen's University offers an enriching and inspiring environment that celebrates knowledge, innovation, and the pursuit of excellence.

Belfast Castle

Perched on the slopes of Cave Hill, Belfast Castle is a majestic and historic landmark that offers breathtaking views of Belfast and its surroundings. With its rich history, stunning architecture, and beautifully landscaped gardens, the castle is a beloved destination for both locals and visitors. It combines historical significance with natural beauty, making it one of Belfast's most cherished attractions.

Historical Background

The current Belfast Castle is actually the third to bear the name. The first Belfast Castle, built in the late 12th century by the Normans, was located in what is now the city center. It was destroyed by fire in 1708. The second castle, a replacement built on the same site, also succumbed to fire in 1708.

The current Belfast Castle was constructed between 1862 and 1870 by the 3rd Marquess of Donegall, who chose to build it in the Scottish Baronial style, which was popular in the Victorian era. The castle was designed by John Lanyon, son of the famous Belfast architect Sir Charles Lanyon. It was intended as a family home and social hub, offering a retreat from the hustle and bustle of city life.

In 1934, the castle and its estate were presented to the City of Belfast by the 9th Earl of Shaftesbury. Since then, it has been maintained by the city and opened to the public as a venue for events, weddings, and tourism.

Architectural Features

Belfast Castle's design is characterized by its Scottish Baronial architecture, featuring turrets, crenellations, and steep gables. The use of sandstone in its construction gives the castle a warm, inviting appearance, and its elevated position provides commanding views over Belfast Lough and the city below.

Inside, the castle boasts richly decorated rooms with period furnishings, offering a glimpse into the Victorian era. The grand staircase, adorned with intricate woodwork and stained glass windows, is one of the most striking features. The rooms and halls are used for various functions and events, maintaining the castle's tradition as a center for social gatherings.

Gardens and Grounds

The castle's grounds are as impressive as the building itself. The beautifully landscaped gardens are meticulously maintained and feature a variety of plants, flowers, and sculptures. The garden's design includes formal terraces, herb gardens, and woodland areas, providing a serene and picturesque setting for visitors to explore.

One of the most charming features of the garden is the Cat Garden, which includes nine cat figures hidden throughout the area, inspired by the legend that good fortune will come to those who find all nine. This adds a playful and engaging element to a stroll through the gardens.

The estate also includes various walking trails that lead through the surrounding parkland and up to Cave Hill. These trails offer stunning views and the opportunity to see local wildlife, making it a popular spot for hikers and nature enthusiasts.

Events and Activities

Belfast Castle is a popular venue for weddings, conferences, and private events, thanks to its picturesque setting and elegant interiors. The castle's catering services and event facilities are renowned for their quality, ensuring that any event held here is memorable.

Throughout the year, the castle hosts a variety of public events, including historical tours, seasonal celebrations, and community activities. These events attract a wide range of visitors and add to the vibrant atmosphere of the castle.

The castle's visitor center provides information about the history of the estate and the surrounding area. It includes exhibits on the archaeology, geology, and history of Cave Hill, enhancing the visitor experience with educational insights.

Community and Cultural Significance

Belfast Castle holds a special place in the hearts of the local community. It is not only a historical landmark but also a venue that brings people together for celebrations, learning, and recreation. The castle's continued use for public and private events ensures that it remains a lively and integral part of Belfast's cultural landscape.

The castle also plays a role in promoting Belfast's heritage and tourism. Its picturesque setting and historical significance make it a key attraction for tourists, contributing to the city's economy and cultural appeal.

Conclusion

Belfast Castle is a jewel in the city's crown, offering a unique blend of history, architecture, and natural beauty. Its stunning location on Cave Hill provides not only breathtaking views but also a connection to Belfast's rich past. Whether you are exploring its grand interiors, wandering through the beautiful gardens, or hiking the scenic trails, a visit to Belfast Castle is a journey into the heart of Belfast's heritage and an experience that captures the essence of its charm and elegance.

Chapter 3:

Natural Beauties

Cave Hill

Cave Hill is one of Belfast's most prominent natural landmarks, offering stunning vistas, rich history, and an array of outdoor activities. Dominating the northern skyline of the city, Cave Hill is easily recognizable by its distinctive profile, often said to resemble the face of a sleeping giant. This picturesque hill provides a perfect escape into nature while being steeped in local folklore and historical significance.

Geological and Natural Features

Cave Hill, part of the Belfast Hills range, rises to a height of 368 meters (1,207 feet) and is composed mainly of basalt, a type of volcanic rock. The hill is named after five caves located on its slopes, which are believed to have been used by early inhabitants for shelter. These caves, along with other natural formations, contribute to the hill's rugged and scenic beauty.

The top of Cave Hill offers panoramic views over Belfast, Belfast Lough, and, on clear days, even the coast of Scotland. The hill's terrain varies from steep cliffs and rocky outcrops to more gentle slopes covered with heathland, grassland, and pockets of woodland. This diversity of habitats supports a wide range of flora and fauna, making it a haven for nature enthusiasts and wildlife watchers.

Historical Significance

Cave Hill has a rich historical heritage, with evidence of human activity dating back thousands of years. One of the most significant historical sites on Cave Hill is McArt's Fort, an ancient ring fort located near the summit. This Iron Age fort, also known as a hillfort, consists of a circular earthwork and offers commanding views of the surrounding landscape. It is believed to have been a defensive stronghold and a place of refuge for early inhabitants.

In addition to McArt's Fort, the area around Cave Hill has yielded numerous archaeological finds, including tools, pottery, and other artifacts from various periods, highlighting its long history of human occupation.

Belfast Castle and Cave Hill

Belfast Castle, located on the lower slopes of Cave Hill, adds to the historical and cultural significance of the area. The castle's grounds extend into the hillside, offering beautifully landscaped gardens and woodland trails that provide access to the hill's natural features. The castle itself, with its stunning architecture and panoramic views, is a key attraction that complements the outdoor experience of Cave Hill.

Outdoor Activities

Cave Hill Country Park is a popular destination for outdoor enthusiasts, offering a variety of trails and activities suitable for all ages and fitness levels. The most well-known trail is the Cave Hill Trail, a circular route that takes hikers past the caves, up to McArt's

Fort, and across the summit, providing breathtaking views and a rewarding challenge.

For those interested in a less strenuous experience, the park offers several shorter trails that wind through the lower slopes and woodland areas. These paths are ideal for leisurely walks, picnics, and birdwatching. The park's diverse habitats support a wide range of bird species, including kestrels, sparrowhawks, and a variety of songbirds.

Rock climbing and bouldering are also popular activities on Cave Hill, with its rocky outcrops providing exciting challenges for climbers. The hill's varied terrain and stunning views make it a favourite spot for photographers and landscape artists.

Folklore and Legends

Cave Hill is steeped in local folklore and legends. The most famous legend is that of Finn McCool, the giant of Irish mythology, who is said to have created the distinctive profile of the hill. The large basaltic outcrop known as McArt's Fort is often referred to as "Napoleon's Nose," due to its resemblance to the profile of the famous French leader.

These legends add a layer of mystique to the hill, capturing the imagination of visitors and connecting the landscape to the rich tapestry of Irish mythology.

Conservation and Community

Cave Hill is managed by Belfast City Council, which works to preserve its natural beauty and historical significance while promoting recreational use. The council collaborates with local community groups, environmental organizations, and volunteers to maintain the trails, protect wildlife habitats, and enhance the visitor experience.

Educational programs and guided tours are offered to help visitors learn about the hill's geology, history, and ecology. These initiatives aim to foster a sense of stewardship and encourage sustainable use of this cherished natural resource.

Conclusion

Cave Hill is a jewel in Belfast's natural landscape, offering a unique combination of outdoor adventure, historical exploration, and breathtaking scenery. Whether you're hiking to the summit for panoramic views, exploring ancient forts and caves, or enjoying a leisurely walk through its woodland trails, Cave Hill provides a memorable and enriching experience. Its blend of natural beauty, rich history, and local legends make it a must-visit destination for anyone exploring Belfast.

Botanic Gardens

The Botanic Gardens in Belfast is one of the city's most treasured green spaces, known for its stunning horticultural displays, historical significance, and vibrant community atmosphere. Situated in the heart of Belfast, near Queen's University, the gardens offer a peaceful retreat from the urban hustle and bustle, while also serving as a hub for cultural events and educational activities.

Historical Background

The Botanic Gardens were established in 1828 by the Belfast Botanic and Horticultural Society, making them one of the oldest public gardens in the United Kingdom. Originally created as a private garden for the members of the society, the gardens were opened to the public in 1895, providing a much-needed green space for the rapidly growing city.

The gardens were designed to showcase a wide variety of plants, both native and exotic, and to promote the study and enjoyment of horticulture. Over the years, they have evolved to include a range of features and attractions that make them a favorite destination for both locals and tourists.

The Palm House

One of the most iconic structures in the Botanic Gardens is the Palm House, a magnificent glasshouse designed by Charles Lanyon and built in stages between 1839 and 1852. The Palm House is one of the earliest examples of a curvilinear cast iron glasshouse, and its design influenced the construction of later Victorian glasshouses, including the famous Kew Gardens Palm House in London.

The Palm House is divided into two wings: the cool wing and the tropical wing. The cool wing features a collection of temperate plants, while the tropical wing houses a variety of exotic species, including towering palms, banana plants, and vibrant orchids. The Palm House provides a warm and humid environment, allowing visitors to experience a tropical oasis in the heart of Belfast.

The Tropical Ravine

Another notable feature of the Botanic Gardens is the Tropical Ravine, a unique Victorian structure built in 1889. Unlike traditional glasshouses, the Tropical Ravine is designed with a sunken garden, allowing visitors to walk along a balcony and look down into the lush, tropical plants below.

The ravine underwent a major restoration project, completed in 2018, to preserve its historical features while updating its facilities for modern visitors. The restored ravine showcases a variety of tropical plants, including ferns, banana trees, and cinnamon plants, along with educational displays about the importance of plant conservation and biodiversity.

Rose Garden and Seasonal Displays

The Botanic Gardens are renowned for their beautiful floral displays, which change with the seasons. The Rose Garden, located near the main entrance, is a highlight during the summer months, featuring a stunning array of rose varieties in full bloom. The garden's carefully curated beds showcase the diversity of roses, from classic hybrid teas to fragrant climbers.

In addition to the Rose Garden, the Botanic Gardens feature a variety of seasonal displays throughout the year. Spring brings a burst of color with tulips, daffodils, and other spring bulbs, while autumn is celebrated with vibrant displays of chrysanthemums and late-blooming perennials. The gardens' horticultural team works diligently to ensure that there is always something in bloom, providing year-round interest for visitors.

The Great Lawn and Bandstand

The Great Lawn is a central feature of the Botanic Gardens, providing an open, grassy area for picnics, relaxation, and outdoor activities. The lawn is surrounded by mature trees and beautifully landscaped beds, creating a serene and picturesque setting.

At one end of the Great Lawn stands the Victorian bandstand, a charming structure that hosts live music performances and community events. The bandstand is a popular spot for local musicians and performers, adding to the lively and welcoming atmosphere of the gardens.

Community and Cultural Events

The Botanic Gardens play a vital role in Belfast's cultural life, hosting a variety of events and festivals throughout the year. The gardens are a key venue for the annual Belfast International Arts Festival, which features performances, exhibitions, and workshops across a range of artistic disciplines.

In addition to the arts festival, the Botanic Gardens host regular events such as plant fairs, craft markets, and family-friendly activities. These events draw large crowds and foster a sense of community, making the gardens a vibrant gathering place for people of all ages.

Educational Programs

As a center for horticultural education, the Botanic Gardens offer a range of programs and workshops for schools, community groups, and the general public. These programs cover topics such as gardening techniques, plant biology, and environmental conservation, helping to inspire a love of plants and nature.

The gardens' educational efforts are supported by a dedicated team of horticulturists and volunteers who share their knowledge and expertise with visitors. Interactive displays, guided tours, and hands-on activities provide engaging learning experiences for all ages.

Conclusion

The Botanic Gardens in Belfast are a cherished green space that combines natural beauty, historical significance, and vibrant community life. Whether you're strolling through the Palm House, exploring the Tropical Ravine, or simply relaxing on the Great Lawn, the gardens offer a peaceful and inspiring escape from the city's bustle. With their rich horticultural heritage, diverse plant collections, and wide range of events and activities, the Botanic Gardens are a must-visit destination for anyone exploring Belfast.

Colin Glen Forest Park

Colin Glen Forest Park is a beautiful and diverse green space located in the southwest of Belfast, offering visitors a wide range of outdoor activities, natural beauty, and educational opportunities. Spanning over 200 acres, this urban forest park is a cherished retreat for both locals and tourists, providing a tranquil escape from city life amidst lush woodlands, rolling meadows, and vibrant wildlife habitats.

Historical Background

The area now known as Colin Glen Forest Park has a rich history, with evidence of human activity dating back to ancient times. The name "Colin" is derived from the Irish "Collan," meaning "wooded valley," reflecting the area's long-standing association with dense forestland. Historically, the parkland was part of the larger Colin Glen Estate, which has seen various uses over the centuries, including agricultural and industrial activities.

In the late 20th century, efforts to preserve and enhance the natural environment led to the establishment of Colin Glen Forest Park. The park was officially opened to the public, providing a protected area for wildlife and a recreational space for the community.

Natural Features and Wildlife

Colin Glen Forest Park is characterized by its diverse landscapes, including ancient woodland, open meadows, rivers, and ponds. The park is home to a wide variety of plant and animal species, making it a haven for nature enthusiasts and wildlife watchers.

The forest is primarily composed of native tree species such as oak, ash, and birch, which provide a rich habitat for birds, mammals, and insects. Visitors may spot red squirrels, badgers, foxes, and a variety of bird species, including songbirds and birds of prey. The park's river, Colin River, supports aquatic life and adds to the area's ecological diversity.

Outdoor Activities

The park offers a wealth of outdoor activities suitable for all ages and fitness levels. Whether you enjoy hiking, cycling, or simply taking a leisurely walk, Colin Glen Forest Park has something to offer.

Hiking and Walking Trails: The park features several well-maintained trails that wind through its varied landscapes. The Bluebell Walk is particularly popular in the spring when the woodland floor is carpeted with bluebells. For those seeking a more challenging hike, the trails leading up to the higher elevations of the park provide stunning views of the surrounding countryside and the Belfast skyline.

Cycling: There are designated cycling paths within the park, allowing visitors to explore the area on two wheels. The trails cater to different skill levels, from easy rides suitable for families to more strenuous routes for experienced cyclists.

Adventure Activities: Colin Glen Forest Park is home to Northern Ireland's first Alpine Coaster, the Black Bull Run, and a state-of-the-art SkyTrek adventure center, which features high ropes courses, zip lines, and climbing walls. These facilities offer exciting and adrenaline-pumping experiences for adventure seekers.

Golf: The park includes a 9-hole golf course, providing a scenic and enjoyable setting for golfers of all abilities. The course is designed to blend seamlessly with the natural landscape, offering a unique golfing experience.

Educational and Community Programs

Colin Glen Forest Park is committed to environmental education and community engagement. The park's visitor center hosts a variety of programs and workshops aimed at raising awareness about conservation and sustainable practices. These educational activities are designed for schools, community groups, and the general public, fostering a deeper appreciation for nature.

The park also offers guided nature walks, wildlife spotting sessions, and hands-on activities such as tree planting and habitat restoration. These programs provide valuable learning experiences and encourage community involvement in preserving the natural environment.

Events and Facilities

Throughout the year, Colin Glen Forest Park hosts a range of events that attract visitors from across Belfast and beyond. These include seasonal festivals, outdoor theater performances, and family-friendly activities. The park's picturesque setting makes it an ideal venue for community gatherings and special occasions.

The park is equipped with facilities to enhance the visitor experience, including picnic areas, playgrounds, and a cafe that offers refreshments and light meals. The visitor center provides information about the park's history, wildlife, and upcoming events, ensuring that visitors can make the most of their visit.

Conservation Efforts

Colin Glen Forest Park is dedicated to the conservation of its natural habitats and the protection of its wildlife. The park's management works closely with environmental organizations and local volunteers to implement conservation projects that enhance biodiversity and maintain the health of the ecosystem.

Initiatives such as reforestation, invasive species control, and water quality monitoring are integral to the park's conservation strategy. These efforts help to preserve the natural beauty of the park and ensure that it remains a thriving habitat for future generations to enjoy.

Conclusion

Colin Glen Forest Park is a gem in Belfast's natural landscape, offering a diverse range of outdoor activities, stunning natural beauty, and rich educational opportunities. Whether you're seeking adventure, relaxation, or a chance to connect with nature, the park provides a welcoming and enriching experience. With its commitment to conservation and community engagement, Colin Glen Forest Park stands as a testament to the value of preserving natural spaces in urban environments, making it a must-visit destination for anyone exploring Belfast.

Ormeau Park

Ormeau Park is Belfast's oldest municipal park and one of its most cherished green spaces. Located along the River Lagan, just south of the city center, the park spans over 100 acres and offers a variety of recreational activities, beautiful landscapes, and historical features. It serves as a vital green lung for the city, providing residents and visitors with a tranquil escape from urban life.

Historical Background

Ormeau Park was officially opened to the public in 1871, making it the first municipal park in Belfast. The land on which the park now stands was originally part of the Donegall estate, a large tract of land owned by the Marquess of Donegall. In the mid-19th century, the Belfast Corporation purchased the land to create a public park, reflecting the Victorian era's emphasis on public health and recreation.

The park's name, "Ormeau," is derived from the French "ormeau," meaning "elm grove," likely referencing the large number of elm trees that once populated the area. The park was designed by the renowned landscape architect Timothy Hevey, who incorporated elements of natural beauty and open space to create a welcoming environment for all.

Landscapes and Features

Ormeau Park is known for its diverse landscapes, including expansive lawns, mature woodlands, and beautifully maintained flower beds. The park's design includes a mix of formal and informal gardens, offering a variety of settings for relaxation and recreation.

One of the park's most notable features is its avenue of trees, which provides a picturesque walkway through the park. These tree-lined paths are particularly beautiful in the spring and autumn, when the foliage displays vibrant colors.

The park also boasts a range of facilities and attractions, including:

Ormeau Embankment: This scenic walkway along the River Lagan offers stunning views of the river and the surrounding landscapes. It is a popular spot for jogging, walking, and cycling.

Bandstand: The historic bandstand, located near the center of the park, is a charming structure that hosts musical performances and community events. It is a focal point for social gatherings and cultural activities.

Playgrounds and Sports Facilities: Ormeau Park is equipped with several playgrounds, providing safe and enjoyable play areas for children. The park also features sports facilities, including tennis courts, basketball courts, and playing fields for football and other sports.

Ormeau Golf Course: Located within the park, the Ormeau Golf Course is one of the oldest golf courses in

Belfast. It offers a challenging yet scenic course for golfers of all skill levels.

Recreational Activities

Ormeau Park is a hub for recreational activities, catering to a wide range of interests and age groups. Whether you are looking for a place to exercise, enjoy nature, or participate in community events, the park has something to offer.

Walking and Running: The park's extensive network of paths and trails makes it ideal for walking, jogging, and running. The routes vary in length and difficulty, accommodating both casual strollers and serious runners.

Cycling: Cyclists can enjoy the park's dedicated cycling paths, which connect to the broader network of bike routes along the River Lagan. The park's flat terrain and scenic views make it a favorite spot for cycling enthusiasts.

Picnicking and Relaxation: With its wide open spaces and shaded areas, Ormeau Park is perfect for picnicking and relaxing. Families and friends often gather here to enjoy outdoor meals and leisurely afternoons.

Birdwatching and Wildlife: The park's diverse habitats support a variety of bird species and other wildlife. Birdwatchers can spot common species such as robins, blackbirds, and woodpeckers, as well as occasional visitors like herons and kingfishers along the river.

Community and Cultural Events

Ormeau Park plays a significant role in Belfast's cultural and community life. The park hosts numerous events throughout the year, including music festivals, outdoor theater performances, and seasonal celebrations. These events attract large crowds and contribute to the vibrant atmosphere of the park.

One of the most popular events is the annual Ormeau Park Fun Day, which features live entertainment, food stalls, games, and activities for all ages. The event fosters a strong sense of community and provides an opportunity for residents to come together and celebrate.

Conservation and Sustainability

Ormeau Park is managed with a focus on conservation and sustainability. Efforts are made to maintain the health of the park's ecosystems, protect wildlife habitats, and promote biodiversity. The park's management team works closely with environmental organizations and local volunteers to implement conservation projects and ensure the long-term preservation of the park.

Conclusion

Ormeau Park is a beloved green space that offers a perfect blend of natural beauty, recreational opportunities, and cultural activities. As Belfast's oldest municipal park, it holds a special place in the hearts of residents and continues to be a vital part of the city's landscape. Whether you are seeking a peaceful retreat, an active day out, or a venue for community events, Ormeau Park provides a welcoming and enriching environment for all. Its rich history, diverse features, and commitment to sustainability make it a must-visit destination for anyone exploring Belfast.

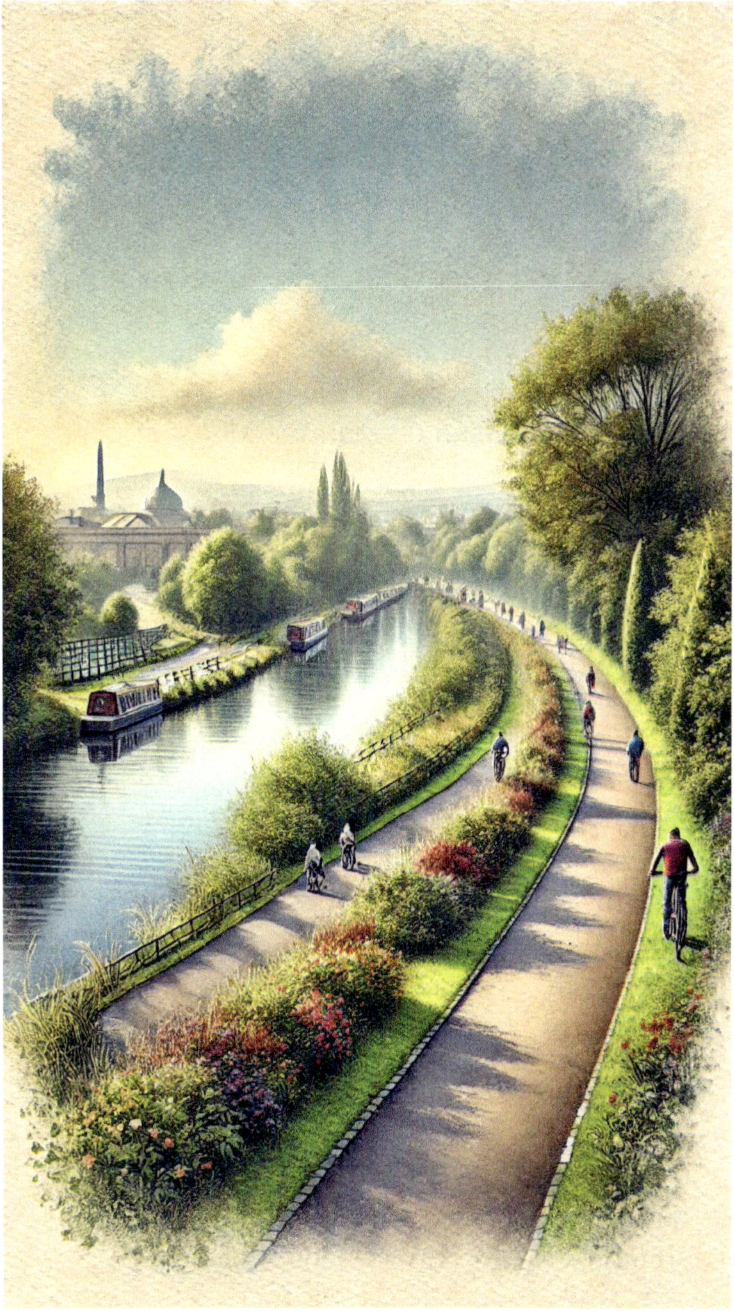

The Lagan Towpath

The Lagan Towpath is a scenic and serene pathway that follows the course of the River Lagan, providing a beautiful escape into nature within easy reach of Belfast city center. Stretching from Belfast to Lisburn, this 11-mile (18-kilometer) route offers picturesque views, diverse wildlife, and a variety of recreational opportunities. Whether you're walking, cycling, or simply enjoying the natural surroundings, the Lagan Towpath is a treasured green corridor that connects urban life with the tranquility of the countryside.

Historical Background

The Lagan Towpath has its origins in the 18th and 19th centuries, when the Lagan Navigation system was developed to facilitate the transport of goods between Belfast and the interior of Ireland. The navigation system included a series of locks, canals, and towpaths, where horses would tow barges along the waterway. The Lagan Navigation played a crucial role in the industrial development of Belfast, allowing for the efficient movement of coal, linen, and other goods.

By the mid-20th century, the advent of rail and road transport led to the decline of the Lagan Navigation. However, the towpath was preserved and repurposed as a recreational route, providing a lasting legacy of the area's industrial past.

Scenic Beauty and Natural Features

The Lagan Towpath is renowned for its scenic beauty, offering a peaceful and picturesque journey through a variety of landscapes. The path meanders alongside the River Lagan, passing through lush woodlands, open meadows, and wetlands. The route is well-maintained, with smooth surfaces and gentle gradients, making it accessible to people of all ages and abilities.

One of the highlights of the towpath is the abundance of wildlife that can be observed along the way. The river and its surrounding habitats support a diverse range of species, including swans, herons, kingfishers, and otters. Birdwatchers and nature enthusiasts will find plenty to enjoy, as the towpath provides excellent opportunities for spotting and photographing wildlife.

Key Points of Interest

Shaw's Bridge: One of the most iconic landmarks along the Lagan Towpath, Shaw's Bridge is an 18th-century stone bridge that spans the River Lagan. The area around the bridge is popular for picnicking, kayaking, and exploring the nearby trails.

Lagan Valley Regional Park: The towpath passes through the Lagan Valley Regional Park, a designated Area of Outstanding Natural Beauty. The park covers over 4,200 acres and offers a variety of recreational activities, including walking, cycling, fishing, and birdwatching. The park's visitor center provides information about the area's natural and cultural heritage.

Giant's Ring: A short detour from the towpath leads to the Giant's Ring, a prehistoric henge monument dating back to around 2700 BCE. This ancient site features a large circular earthwork and a central burial chamber, offering a fascinating glimpse into the region's early history.

Lisburn: The towpath terminates in the town of Lisburn, which boasts a variety of attractions, including the Irish Linen Centre and Lisburn Museum, showcasing the history of linen production in the area. Lisburn's bustling market square and charming shops provide a pleasant end point for the journey.

Recreational Activities

The Lagan Towpath is a haven for outdoor enthusiasts, offering a wide range of recreational activities:

Walking and Hiking: The towpath is ideal for leisurely strolls, brisk walks, and long-distance hikes. The well-marked route and gentle terrain make it suitable for walkers of all levels.

Cycling: Cyclists can enjoy a scenic ride along the towpath, with designated cycle paths ensuring a safe and enjoyable experience. Bike rentals are available in Belfast and Lisburn for those who do not have their own bicycles.

Running and Jogging: The smooth and flat surface of the towpath makes it a popular spot for running and jogging, providing a continuous and uninterrupted route through picturesque surroundings. Runners can enjoy the fresh air and scenic views while getting in their exercise.

Fishing: The River Lagan is home to a variety of fish species, making it a popular spot for angling. Fishing permits are required and can be obtained from local authorities. The tranquil setting along the towpath provides an ideal environment for a relaxing day of fishing.

Boating and Kayaking: Sections of the River Lagan are suitable for boating and kayaking. The calm waters and natural beauty of the river offer a serene paddling experience. Shaw's Bridge is a particularly popular launch point for kayakers.

Community and Cultural Events

The Lagan Towpath is more than just a recreational route; it is also a vibrant community space. Throughout the year, various events and activities are organized along the towpath, fostering a sense of community and encouraging outdoor engagement. These events include nature walks, guided tours, charity runs, and cultural festivals.

Seasonal activities, such as springtime bluebell walks and autumn foliage tours, highlight the changing beauty of the towpath and attract visitors who appreciate the natural rhythms of the landscape.

Conservation and Sustainability

The Lagan Towpath is managed with a strong emphasis on conservation and sustainability. Efforts are made to preserve the natural habitats and wildlife that thrive along the route. The Lagan Valley Regional Park and other conservation organizations work together to protect the ecological integrity of the area, ensuring that it remains a haven for both people and nature.

Educational programs and initiatives, such as litter clean-ups and wildlife monitoring, involve the local community in the stewardship of the towpath. These efforts help to maintain the path's pristine condition and promote environmental awareness.

Visitor Information

The Lagan Towpath is easily accessible from several points in Belfast and Lisburn. Parking facilities are available at key access points, and public transportation options make it convenient for visitors to reach the towpath.

Amenities along the route include rest areas, picnic spots, and informational signage that provides insights into the history, wildlife, and points of interest along the way. The visitor center at Lagan Valley Regional Park offers additional resources, including maps, guides, and information about upcoming events.

Conclusion

The Lagan Towpath is a cherished green corridor that connects the bustling urban environment of Belfast with the serene countryside of Lisburn. Its rich history, natural beauty, and wide range of recreational opportunities make it a must-visit destination for anyone seeking to explore the outdoors in Northern Ireland. Whether you are walking, cycling, fishing, or simply enjoying the scenic views, the Lagan Towpath offers a peaceful and enriching experience that showcases the best of Belfast's natural heritage.

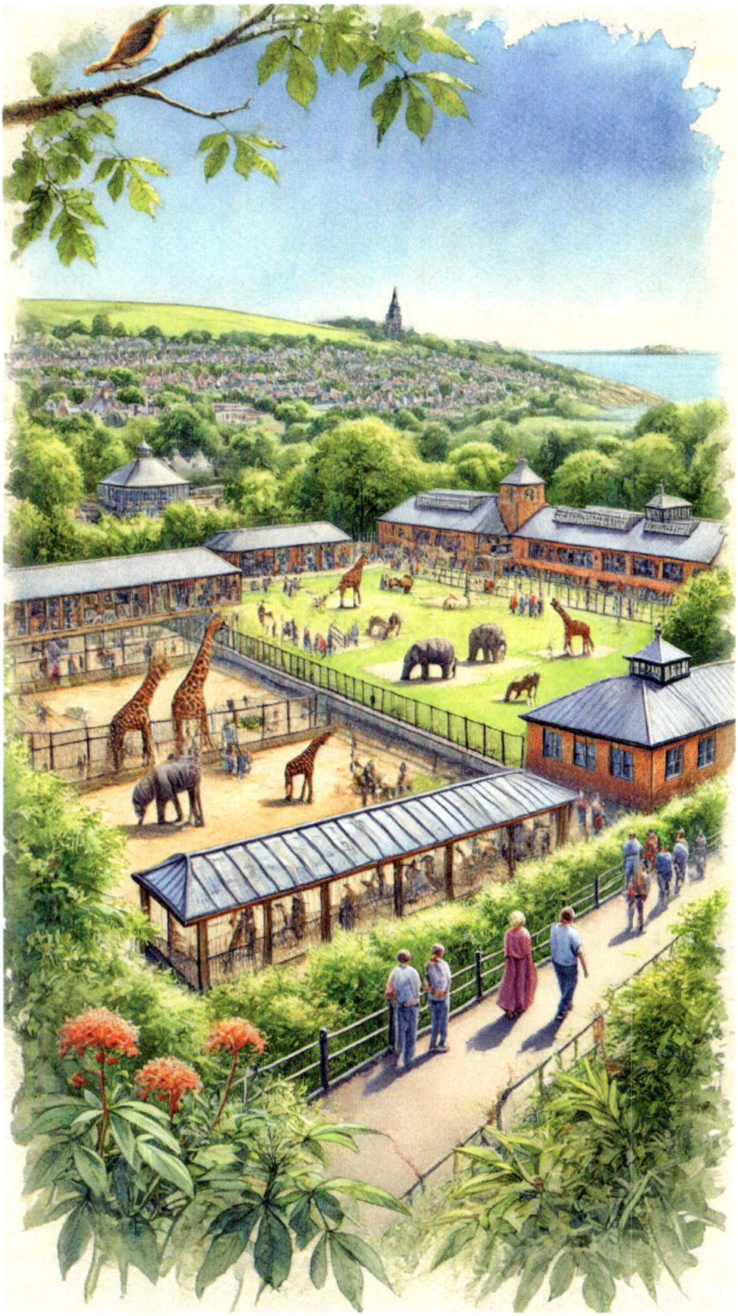

Belfast Zoo

Belfast Zoo is one of the city's most popular attractions, offering a captivating experience for visitors of all ages. Located on the slopes of Cave Hill, the zoo provides stunning views over Belfast Lough and the city. Home to more than 120 species of animals, many of which are endangered or rare, Belfast Zoo plays a crucial role in conservation, education, and recreation.

Historical Background

Belfast Zoo was officially opened in 1934, making it one of the oldest zoos in Northern Ireland. The zoo was established on the grounds of Bellevue, a former estate that provided an ideal location due to its natural landscape and expansive views. Over the decades, the zoo has evolved significantly, expanding its facilities and animal collection to become a leading institution for wildlife conservation.

During its early years, Belfast Zoo faced many challenges, including the impact of World War II, when resources were scarce, and the zoo had to make do with limited supplies. However, the dedication of the staff and the support of the local community helped the zoo to survive and thrive.

Animal Collection

Belfast Zoo is home to a diverse range of animals from around the world. The zoo's collection includes mammals, birds, reptiles, amphibians, and invertebrates, providing visitors with a comprehensive glimpse into the animal kingdom. Some of the key exhibits and species include:

Asian Elephants: The zoo's elephant enclosure is one of its most popular attractions, featuring spacious habitats designed to mimic the natural environment of these majestic animals. The zoo participates in international breeding programs to help conserve Asian elephants, which are endangered in the wild.

Giraffe and Zebra: The African Savannah exhibit showcases the zoo's giraffes and zebras, offering visitors the chance to observe these graceful creatures up close. The exhibit is designed to provide a naturalistic setting that encourages natural behaviors.

Primates: Belfast Zoo is home to several species of primates, including chimpanzees, spider monkeys, and lemurs. The primate enclosures are designed to stimulate the animals' intelligence and curiosity, featuring climbing structures, ropes, and enrichment activities.

Big Cats: The zoo's big cat exhibits include lions, tigers, and snow leopards. These enclosures are carefully designed to provide a safe and enriching environment for the animals, while also offering visitors an exciting viewing experience.

Birds: The aviaries at Belfast Zoo house a variety of bird species, from colorful parrots to majestic birds of prey. The zoo's bird collection highlights the incredible diversity of avian life and includes several endangered species.

Reptiles and Amphibians: The Reptile House features a fascinating collection of snakes, lizards, frogs, and other reptiles and amphibians. Visitors can learn about the unique adaptations and behaviors of these cold-blooded creatures.

Conservation and Research

Belfast Zoo is deeply committed to wildlife conservation and plays an active role in various breeding and research programs. The zoo collaborates with other zoos and conservation organizations worldwide to protect endangered species and promote biodiversity. Some of the key conservation initiatives include:

Breeding Programs: The zoo participates in European Endangered Species Programs (EEP) and other international breeding initiatives to help ensure the survival of threatened species. These programs involve careful management of genetic diversity and collaboration between zoos to breed healthy populations.

Habitat Conservation: Belfast Zoo supports habitat conservation projects in the wild, working to protect the natural environments of the species it houses. These efforts include funding anti-poaching initiatives, habitat restoration, and community-based conservation programs.

Research: The zoo conducts research on animal behavior, health, and genetics, contributing valuable knowledge to the field of zoology. This research helps improve the care and management of animals in captivity and supports conservation efforts in the wild.

Education and Outreach

Education is a central mission of Belfast Zoo, and the facility offers a range of programs and resources to engage and inform visitors. These educational initiatives include:

School Programs: The zoo provides educational workshops and tours for school groups, aligned with the curriculum to enhance students' understanding of biology, ecology, and conservation. Hands-on activities and interactive exhibits make learning fun and memorable.

Public Talks and Demonstrations: Regular talks and feeding demonstrations by zookeepers give visitors insights into the animals' lives and the work involved in caring for them. These sessions also highlight important conservation messages.

Outreach Programs: The zoo's outreach team visits schools, community groups, and events to deliver educational presentations and activities. These programs extend the zoo's educational impact beyond its gates and foster a broader appreciation for wildlife.

Visitor Experience

Belfast Zoo offers a range of amenities and services to ensure a comfortable and enjoyable visit for all guests. The zoo's facilities include:

Cafe and Picnic Areas: The zoo's cafe offers a variety of refreshments and meals, while picnic areas provide scenic spots for visitors to relax and enjoy their own food.

Play Areas: The zoo features several play areas for children, including adventure playgrounds and interactive exhibits. These areas are designed to entertain and engage young visitors.

Gift Shop: The zoo's gift shop offers a selection of souvenirs, toys, and educational materials, allowing visitors to take home a memento of their visit.

Accessibility: Belfast Zoo is committed to accessibility, with wheelchair-friendly paths, accessible restrooms, and other facilities to ensure that all visitors can enjoy their experience.

Conclusion

Belfast Zoo is a beloved institution that combines the beauty of nature with the importance of conservation and education. Its diverse animal collection, commitment to wildlife preservation, and engaging educational programs make it a must-visit destination for anyone interested in the natural world. Set against the stunning backdrop of Cave Hill, the zoo offers a unique and enriching experience that inspires a deeper appreciation for wildlife and the environment. Whether you're a family, a school group, or a solo traveler, a visit to Belfast Zoo promises to be a memorable and enlightening adventure.

Chapter 4:

Hidden Gems

Secret Gardens and Courtyards

Belfast is a city filled with hidden gems, including a variety of secret gardens and courtyards that offer tranquil escapes from the urban hustle and bustle. These charming spots are often tucked away behind buildings, accessible through narrow passageways, or hidden in plain sight. They provide serene settings for relaxation, reflection, and enjoying nature amidst the city's vibrant environment.

Botanic Gardens Hidden Corners

While the Botanic Gardens is well-known and frequently visited, it has several secluded areas that offer a quieter, more intimate experience. Beyond the main attractions like the Palm House and Tropical Ravine, you can find hidden corners filled with rare plants, shaded benches, and peaceful pathways. The garden's less-traveled paths are perfect for a solitary stroll or a quiet read under the trees.

The Walled Garden at Sir Thomas and Lady Dixon Park

Sir Thomas and Lady Dixon Park is famous for its International Rose Garden, but it also houses a beautiful walled garden that is a bit off the beaten path. This garden is meticulously maintained, featuring a stunning array of flowers, herbaceous borders, and a charming fountain. The high brick walls provide a sense of seclusion, making it an ideal spot for relaxation and contemplation.

Victoria Square Rooftop Garden

Victoria Square Shopping Centre is not only a retail hub but also home to a hidden rooftop garden. This urban oasis offers panoramic views of Belfast and a peaceful retreat amidst the city's bustling shopping district. The garden features a variety of plants and seating areas, providing a green space for visitors to unwind and enjoy the skyline.

St. George's Gardens

Located behind St. George's Church in the High Street area, St. George's Gardens is a lesser-known green space that offers a peaceful respite in the city center. This garden features well-kept lawns, flowerbeds, and mature trees, along with benches where visitors can sit and enjoy the tranquility. It's a perfect spot for a quiet lunch break or a moment of reflection away from the busy streets.

Linen Hall Library Courtyard

The Linen Hall Library, one of Belfast's cultural treasures, houses a hidden courtyard that offers a quiet retreat for visitors. Surrounded by historic buildings, this courtyard features seating areas and a variety of plants, creating a serene environment for reading or enjoying a cup of coffee. The library itself is a fascinating place to explore, with its extensive collections and historical significance.

Queen's University Belfast Cloisters and Gardens

Queen's University Belfast is not only an academic institution but also a place of architectural and botanical beauty. The university's cloisters and surrounding gardens provide peaceful retreats with lush greenery, flowerbeds, and picturesque walkways. The quadrangles and courtyards within the university grounds are perfect for a leisurely stroll or a relaxing break amidst beautiful surroundings.

Belfast Castle Gardens

Belfast Castle, situated on the slopes of Cave Hill, is surrounded by beautifully landscaped gardens that offer stunning views over the city. While the castle itself is a popular attraction, the gardens feature several hidden spots, including a Japanese-style garden, secluded benches, and woodland trails. These areas provide a tranquil setting for exploring nature and enjoying the scenic beauty of Belfast.

The Dark Horse Courtyard

In the heart of the Cathedral Quarter, The Dark Horse is a charming pub with a hidden courtyard that is a true gem. Decorated with murals and artwork, this courtyard offers a cozy and atmospheric setting for enjoying a drink or meal. The unique decor and secluded feel make it a favorite spot for locals and visitors alike.

Belfast Botanic Gardens Tropical Ravine

While not exactly a secret, the Tropical Ravine in the Botanic Gardens offers a hidden world of exotic plants and lush greenery. Recently restored, this Victorian structure allows visitors to walk along balconies and look down into a ravine filled with tropical plants, waterfalls, and pools. It's a fascinating and serene environment that transports you to a different world.

Conclusion

Belfast's secret gardens and courtyards are enchanting spots that provide a welcome escape from the city's energetic pace. Each hidden gem offers its own unique charm, whether it's the historical ambiance of a university cloister, the urban greenery of a rooftop garden, or the peaceful retreat of a walled garden. Exploring these secret spaces reveals a different side of Belfast, one filled with tranquility, beauty, and the joy of discovering hidden treasures.

Murals and Street Art

Belfast is renowned for its vibrant murals and street art, which have become a significant part of the city's cultural landscape. These artworks reflect Belfast's complex history, political struggles, social issues, and cultural pride. They transform the city's walls into a dynamic open-air gallery, attracting visitors from around the world who come to explore and understand the stories behind these compelling visual narratives.

Historical Background

The tradition of mural painting in Belfast dates back to the early 20th century, but it gained significant momentum during the Troubles, a period of conflict in Northern Ireland from the late 1960s to 1998. Murals became a means of expression for both unionist and nationalist communities, conveying political messages, commemorating historical events, and honoring individuals.

In recent years, the focus of Belfast's street art has shifted from political themes to include a broader range of subjects, such as social issues, cultural heritage, and artistic expression. This evolution reflects the city's ongoing journey towards peace and reconciliation, and its desire to celebrate a shared identity.

Key Locations and Themes

The Falls Road

The Falls Road is one of the most famous locations for political murals in Belfast. This predominantly nationalist area features murals that commemorate the Irish struggle for independence, honor hunger strikers, and celebrate Irish culture and identity. Notable murals include tributes to Bobby Sands and other members of the Provisional Irish Republican Army (IRA).

The Shankill Road

In contrast to the Falls Road, the Shankill Road is a predominantly unionist area with murals that reflect loyalist perspectives. These murals often depict historical events related to the Ulster Volunteer Force (UVF) and the Ulster Defence Association (UDA), as well as symbols of British identity and loyalty to the Crown. The murals here provide insight into the unionist community's history and values.

The Peace Walls

The Peace Walls, which separate nationalist and unionist neighborhoods, are themselves canvases for a variety of artworks. These walls were initially erected to prevent violence between communities, but they have since become a space for artistic expression, featuring messages of peace, hope, and reconciliation from both local and international artists.

The Cathedral Quarter

The Cathedral Quarter is the cultural heart of Belfast and home to some of the city's most vibrant and creative street art. Unlike the political murals of the Falls and Shankill Roads, the art in this area tends to be more diverse in theme, including abstract designs, portraits, and contemporary pieces. The annual Hit the North street art festival brings together local and international artists to create new works, making the area a constantly evolving gallery.

The International Wall

Located near Divis Street, the International Wall is a prominent site for political and social commentary. The murals here address global issues such as apartheid, Palestinian rights, and social justice movements. The wall serves as a platform for solidarity and international awareness, reflecting Belfast's connection to global struggles.

East Belfast

East Belfast has seen a surge in street art, with many murals celebrating the area's industrial heritage, cultural icons, and local history. Notable artworks include murals dedicated to the shipyard workers of Harland & Wolff, where the RMS Titanic was built, and tributes to famous East Belfast natives such as C.S. Lewis and George Best.

Contemporary Street Art and Artists

The contemporary street art scene in Belfast is vibrant and diverse, with artists exploring a wide range of themes beyond the political. Some of the city's most notable street artists include:

Dan Kitchener (DANK): Known for his vibrant, neon-infused cityscapes, DANK's murals add a splash of color and modernity to Belfast's urban landscape. His work often depicts bustling urban scenes, illuminated by rain and artificial light.

Emic: Emic's murals often focus on social and cultural themes, blending portraiture with intricate patterns and bold colors. His work can be seen in various locations across Belfast, adding depth and character to the city's streets.

Friz: A prominent female artist in the Belfast street art scene, Friz is known for her ethereal and nature-inspired murals. Her work often features strong, feminine figures intertwined with elements of the natural world, creating a sense of mysticism and beauty.

Maser: Originally from Dublin, Maser's work has made a significant impact in Belfast. His abstract and geometric designs are instantly recognizable, bringing a contemporary and graphic quality to the city's street art.

Street Art Tours

To fully appreciate the depth and diversity of Belfast's murals and street art, guided tours are available. These tours are led by knowledgeable guides who provide context and insights into the history and meaning behind the artworks. Popular tours include:

Belfast Mural Tours: These tours focus on the political murals of the Falls and Shankill Roads, offering a detailed look at the history and stories behind the artworks.

Seedhead Arts Street Art Walking Tour: This tour explores the contemporary street art scene in the Cathedral Quarter and beyond, highlighting the work of local and international artists.

Conclusion

Belfast's murals and street art are more than just visual spectacles; they are a powerful form of storytelling that captures the city's complex history, cultural identity, and evolving social landscape. From the politically charged murals of the Troubles to the vibrant and diverse contemporary artworks, these pieces offer a unique and immersive way to experience Belfast. Whether you're a local or a visitor, exploring Belfast's murals and street art provides a profound and engaging journey through the city's past, present, and future.

Hidden Cafes and Bistros

Belfast is home to a variety of charming and unique cafes and bistros, many of which are tucked away in quiet corners, offering a cozy and intimate atmosphere. These hidden gems provide the perfect retreat for a relaxing coffee, a leisurely brunch, or a delicious meal, often accompanied by delightful decor and a warm, welcoming vibe. Here are some of the best-hidden cafes and bistros in Belfast that you might want to discover.

Established Coffee

Location: 54 Hill Street, Cathedral Quarter

Nestled in the heart of the Cathedral Quarter, Established Coffee is a haven for coffee lovers. Known for its minimalist design and industrial chic decor, this cafe offers a range of expertly brewed coffees, teas, and a menu of seasonal and locally sourced food. The atmosphere is laid-back, making it an ideal spot to relax, read, or catch up with friends. Despite its popularity, its tucked-away location gives it a hidden gem feel.

The Pocket

Location: 69 University Road, near Queen's University

Located near Queen's University, The Pocket is a small but vibrant cafe that caters to students and locals alike. Its bright, modern interior is complemented by a menu that features specialty coffee, innovative brunch options, and delicious baked goods. The Pocket's proximity to the university and Botanic Gardens makes it a perfect spot for a quiet study session or a break from a leisurely walk in the park.

Harlem Cafe

Location: 34 Bedford Street, near City Hall

Harlem Cafe, just a short walk from Belfast City Hall, is a quirky and eclectic spot with a distinctive vintage charm. The cafe's interior is adorned with mismatched furniture, artwork, and antiques, creating a warm and inviting atmosphere. The menu is diverse, offering everything from hearty breakfasts and light lunches to decadent cakes and desserts. Its hidden location on Bedford Street makes it a delightful surprise for those who stumble upon it.

Kaffe O

Location: 73 Ormeau Road, Ormeau

Kaffe O brings a taste of Scandinavia to Belfast, offering a menu inspired by Danish cafe culture. Located on Ormeau Road, this hidden gem is known for its minimalist decor, organic coffee, and healthy food options. The cafe's relaxed ambiance and focus on quality ingredients make it a favorite among those looking for a calm and refreshing cafe experience.

The National Grande Cafe

Location: 62 High Street, Cathedral Quarter

Tucked away in a courtyard off High Street, The National Grande Cafe is part of The National, a popular bar and restaurant in the Cathedral Quarter. The cafe offers a tranquil escape from the bustling streets outside, with a stylish interior and a beautiful outdoor seating area. The menu includes a range of coffees, teas, pastries, and light meals, making it an excellent spot for a leisurely afternoon.

General Merchants

Location: 481 Ormeau Road, Ormeau

General Merchants on Ormeau Road is a hidden gem that combines a contemporary cafe vibe with a nod to Belfast's mercantile history. The cafe's interior is modern and welcoming, featuring reclaimed wood and industrial accents. The menu is innovative and diverse, with a focus on fresh, locally sourced ingredients. From creative brunch dishes to specialty coffee, General Merchants offers a delightful dining experience.

Town Square

Location: 45 Botanic Avenue, near Botanic Gardens

Located on Botanic Avenue, near Queen's University and Botanic Gardens, Town Square is a popular spot among students and locals. The cafe features a modern, open-plan design with plenty of natural light and comfortable seating. The menu includes a wide range of coffees, teas, and a selection of delicious meals, from breakfast and brunch to evening bites. Despite its central location, Town Square maintains a cozy and intimate atmosphere.

The Jailhouse

Location: 5 Joy's Entry, near High Street

The Jailhouse is a hidden gem located in one of Belfast's historic entries, Joy's Entry. This unique cafe and bar is housed in a building that once served as a holding cell for prisoners. The interior retains much of its historical charm, with exposed brick walls, wooden beams, and vintage decor. The menu offers a variety of drinks, light bites, and hearty meals, making it a great spot for a relaxed drink or a casual meal.

5A Coffee

Location: 5A Lockview Road, Stranmillis

Tucked away in the Stranmillis area, 5A Coffee is a small, independent cafe known for its high-quality coffee and cozy atmosphere. The cafe's minimalist decor and friendly staff create a welcoming environment, perfect for enjoying a quiet coffee or catching up with friends. The menu features specialty coffees, teas, and a selection of homemade pastries and snacks.

The Black Box Cafe

Location: 18-22 Hill Street, Cathedral Quarter

Situated within The Black Box arts venue, The Black Box Cafe offers a creative and laid-back environment. The cafe is a hidden gem in the Cathedral Quarter, known for its eclectic decor and vibrant atmosphere. It serves a variety of coffees, teas, and light meals, making it a perfect spot to relax before or after attending one of the venue's many events, including live music, theater, and comedy shows.

Conclusion

Belfast's hidden cafes and bistros offer a delightful escape from the hustle and bustle of city life. Each of these unique spots provides a cozy and inviting atmosphere, along with delicious food and drink options. Whether you're looking for a quiet place to work, a comfortable spot to catch up with friends, or simply a new place to explore, these hidden gems are sure to provide a memorable and enjoyable experience.

Off-the-Beaten-Path Museums

Belfast is home to a variety of unique and lesser-known museums that offer fascinating insights into the city's rich history, culture, and industrial heritage. These off-the-beaten-path museums provide visitors with the opportunity to explore niche subjects, discover hidden stories, and gain a deeper understanding of Belfast beyond its more famous attractions. Here are some of the best off-the-beaten-path museums in Belfast that are worth exploring.

The War Memorial Museum

Location: Talbot Street, Cathedral Quarter

The Northern Ireland War Memorial Museum is a hidden gem located in the Cathedral Quarter. This small but significant museum is dedicated to the memory of those who served in the First and Second World Wars. The museum features exhibits on the Belfast Blitz, the role of women during the war, and the impact of the war on Northern Ireland. Visitors can explore artifacts, photographs, and personal stories that bring to life the experiences of those who lived through these tumultuous times.

The Museum of Orange Heritage

Location: Schomberg House, Cregagh Road

The Museum of Orange Heritage at Schomberg House offers an in-depth look at the history and traditions of the Orange Order, one of Northern Ireland's most influential fraternal organizations. The museum's exhibits cover a range of topics, including the origins of the Orange Order, its role in the history of Ireland, and its cultural and social impact. Visitors can explore a collection of artifacts, banners, and regalia, as well as interactive displays that provide a comprehensive understanding of this unique institution.

The Irish Republican History Museum

Location: Conway Mill, Conway Street

Housed in the historic Conway Mill, the Irish Republican History Museum is dedicated to the history of Irish republicanism and the struggle for Irish independence. The museum features a wide range of exhibits, including documents, photographs, and personal items related to key events and figures in the republican movement. Highlights include displays on the 1916 Easter Rising, the Irish War of Independence, and the Troubles. The museum provides a valuable perspective on the political and social history of Northern Ireland.

The Transport Museum

Location: Cultra, County Down (short drive from Belfast)

The Ulster Transport Museum, located a short drive from Belfast, offers a fascinating exploration of Northern Ireland's transport heritage. The museum's extensive collection includes vintage cars, steam locomotives, buses, and trams, as well as exhibits on shipbuilding and aviation. Visitors can learn about the development of transportation in Northern Ireland and its impact on the region's economy and society. The museum is part of the Ulster Folk & Transport Museum, which also features an outdoor folk museum with historic buildings and living history demonstrations.

The Flame Gasworks Museum

Location: Carrickfergus, County Antrim (short drive from Belfast)

Located in Carrickfergus, a short drive from Belfast, the Flame Gasworks Museum is one of the last remaining coal gasworks in Europe. The museum offers a unique glimpse into the history of gas production and its role in urban development. Visitors can explore the original buildings and machinery used to produce coal gas, as well as exhibits on the science and technology behind gasworks. The museum also features a visitor center with interactive displays and educational programs.

The Linen Hall Library

Location: Donegall Square North, City Center

While primarily a library, the Linen Hall Library also functions as a museum of Belfast's literary and cultural history. Founded in 1788, it is the oldest library in Belfast and houses an extensive collection of books, manuscripts, and artifacts related to Irish literature, politics, and history. The library's special collections include rare editions of works by famous Irish writers, as well as materials related to the Troubles and the Irish language. The library's exhibitions and events provide a deeper understanding of Belfast's literary heritage.

The Royal Ulster Rifles Museum

Location: Waring Street, Cathedral Quarter

The Royal Ulster Rifles Museum is a small but fascinating museum dedicated to the history of the Royal Ulster Rifles, an infantry regiment of the British Army. The museum's exhibits cover the regiment's involvement in various conflicts, including the First and Second World Wars, the Korean War, and the Troubles. Visitors can explore a collection of uniforms, medals, weapons, and personal items that tell the story of the regiment and its soldiers. The museum provides a unique perspective on military history and the experiences of those who served.

The HMS Caroline

Location: Alexandra Dock, Titanic Quarter

HMS Caroline is a decommissioned C-class light cruiser of the Royal Navy that has been preserved as a museum ship in the Titanic Quarter. Launched in 1914, HMS Caroline saw service during the First World War and is one of the last surviving ships from the Battle of Jutland. Visitors can explore the ship's decks, engine room, and living quarters, as well as interactive exhibits that provide insights into naval history and life at sea.

The ship offers a unique and immersive experience for history enthusiasts and maritime aficionados.

Conclusion

Belfast's off-the-beaten-path museums offer a wealth of opportunities to explore the city's diverse history, culture, and heritage. From military and political history to transportation and literary heritage, these hidden gems provide fascinating insights and unique experiences. Whether you are a history buff, a cultural enthusiast, or simply curious about Belfast's past, these lesser-known museums are well worth a visit.

Lesser-Known Pubs in Belfast

Belfast is famous for its lively pub scene, with many well-known establishments like The Crown Liquor Saloon and Kelly's Cellars drawing large crowds. However, the city is also home to a number of lesser-known pubs that offer unique atmospheres, rich histories, and welcoming vibes. These hidden gems provide a more intimate and often authentic experience, making them perfect spots for those looking to enjoy a pint away from the tourist trails. Here are some of Belfast's best lesser-known pubs that are worth discovering.

The John Hewitt

Location: 51 Donegall Street, Cathedral Quarter

Named after the famous Belfast poet and socialist John Hewitt, this pub is a favorite among locals for its cultural vibe and vibrant atmosphere. The John Hewitt is owned by the Belfast Unemployed Resource Centre, and all profits go towards supporting the center's community projects. The pub features regular live music, poetry readings, and art exhibitions, making it a cultural hub in the Cathedral Quarter. With its extensive selection of local ales and craft beers, The John Hewitt offers a warm and welcoming environment for anyone looking to enjoy Belfast's creative spirit.

The Sunflower

Location: 65 Union Street, City Center

The Sunflower is easily recognizable by the security cage around its entrance, a relic from the Troubles that adds a unique historical touch to the pub. Inside, you'll find a cozy and eclectic space filled with local artwork and friendly patrons. The Sunflower is known for its excellent selection of craft beers, ciders, and traditional Irish music sessions. The pub also has a spacious beer garden, perfect for enjoying a pint on a sunny day. Its relaxed and unpretentious atmosphere makes it a hidden gem in the heart of the city.

The Jeggy Nettle

Location: 7 Stranmillis Road, Stranmillis

Located in the Stranmillis area, The Jeggy Nettle is a modern pub with a laid-back vibe. It's a favorite among students and locals alike, thanks to its comfortable setting, friendly staff, and excellent food. The pub's menu features a variety of delicious dishes, including vegan and vegetarian options, alongside a well-curated selection of craft beers and cocktails. The Jeggy Nettle also hosts regular quiz nights, live music, and other events, making it a lively and engaging place to visit.

The Deer's Head

Location: 1-3 Lower Garfield Street, City Center

The Deer's Head is one of Belfast's oldest pubs, recently revitalized with its own microbrewery, Bell's Brewery, located on-site. The pub retains much of its original charm, with traditional decor and a warm, welcoming atmosphere. Visitors can enjoy a range of house-brewed beers, as well as a selection of local and international ales. The Deer's Head also features live music and events, adding to its vibrant ambiance. Its historical significance and unique offerings make it a must-visit for beer enthusiasts and history buffs alike.

Bittles Bar

Location: 70 Upper Church Lane, City Center

Tucked away in a narrow alley, Bittles Bar is a distinctive triangular-shaped pub that's hard to miss once you find it. Known for its cozy and intimate setting, Bittles Bar boasts an impressive collection of whiskeys and local ales. The walls are adorned with artwork depicting Irish literary figures and political icons, reflecting the pub's rich cultural heritage. Its quirky shape and off-the-beaten-path location make Bittles Bar a unique spot to enjoy a quiet drink and soak in Belfast's history.

The Duke of York

Location: 7-11 Commercial Court, Cathedral Quarter

While not entirely unknown, The Duke of York is often overshadowed by some of the more famous pubs in the area. This charming pub is located in a cobbled alleyway in the Cathedral Quarter and offers a traditional Belfast pub experience. With its wood-paneled interiors, antique decor, and extensive whiskey selection, The Duke of York exudes character and history. The pub is also known for its vibrant beer garden, which is beautifully decorated with murals and fairy lights, creating a magical atmosphere in the evenings.

The Errigle Inn

Location: 312-320 Ormeau Road, Ormeau

The Errigle Inn is a beloved neighborhood pub located on the Ormeau Road. With its multiple bars, rooftop terrace, and live music venue, the Errigle Inn offers something for everyone. The pub has a long history dating back to the 1930s and is known for its friendly service and welcoming environment. Whether you're looking for a quiet spot to enjoy a pint or a lively place to watch a match, the Errigle Inn has you covered. Its diverse range of beers, ciders, and spirits, along with its hearty pub grub, make it a favorite among locals.

The Reporter

Location: 12 Union Street, City Center

The Reporter is a hidden gem that pays homage to Belfast's rich journalistic heritage. The pub's decor includes vintage typewriters, newspapers, and press-related memorabilia, creating a unique and nostalgic atmosphere. The Reporter offers a great selection of craft beers, cocktails, and wines, along with a menu of delicious tapas and sharing plates. Its cozy and intimate setting, combined with its historical theme, makes The Reporter a perfect spot for a quiet drink or a relaxed evening out.

The Pavilion Bar

Location: 296 Ormeau Road, Ormeau

Known locally as "The Big House," The Pavilion Bar is a spacious and vibrant pub located on the Ormeau Road. The pub features multiple floors, each with its own unique atmosphere, from the lively main bar to the more intimate upstairs lounge. The Pavilion is popular for its live music events, quiz nights, and comedy shows, making it a hub of entertainment. The pub's extensive drinks menu includes a variety of beers, wines, and spirits, as well as delicious food options. Its friendly and lively atmosphere makes it a great place to socialize and enjoy a night out.

The Parador

Location: 116-118 Ormeau Road, Ormeau

The Parador is a classic Belfast pub with a welcoming and unpretentious vibe. Located on the Ormeau Road, this pub is known for its friendly staff, regular live music, and lively atmosphere. The Parador offers a range of beers, ciders, and spirits, along with traditional pub fare. Its cozy interiors and local clientele make it a perfect spot to experience authentic Belfast hospitality. Whether you're stopping by for a quick drink or spending an evening enjoying the music, The Parador provides a warm and enjoyable experience.

Conclusion

Belfast's lesser-known pubs offer a diverse and authentic pub experience away from the more touristy spots. Each of these hidden gems has its own unique charm, from cultural hubs and historical landmarks to modern hangouts and cozy retreats. Whether you're a local looking for a new favorite spot or a visitor seeking to explore the city's pub scene, these lesser-known pubs provide a delightful and memorable experience.

Chapter 5: Day Trips and Excursions

The Gobbins Cliff Path

The Gobbins Cliff Path is a dramatic and exhilarating coastal walk located along the Causeway Coastal Route in County Antrim, Northern Ireland. This unique and adventurous path offers stunning views, thrilling experiences, and a deep connection to the natural beauty of the Irish coastline. Originally built in the early 20th century, the Gobbins has been carefully restored and reopened to the public, providing an unforgettable experience for those who visit.

Historical Background

The Gobbins Cliff Path was the brainchild of Berkeley Deane Wise, a pioneering railway engineer and visionary. In 1902, Wise began construction on the path as a means to boost tourism and provide a unique attraction along the scenic coastline. The original path, which opened in 1902, featured a series of bridges, tunnels, and walkways carved directly into the basalt cliffs.

The Gobbins quickly became a popular destination, drawing visitors from far and wide to experience the thrill of walking along the sheer cliffs and taking in the breathtaking views. However, due to maintenance challenges and safety concerns, the path eventually fell into disrepair and was closed in the 1950s.

In the early 21st century, efforts were made to restore the Gobbins Cliff Path to its former glory. After extensive renovation work, the path was reopened in

2015, offering a modern and safe version of the original experience while preserving the historical and natural essence of the site.

The Walk

The Gobbins Cliff Path is a guided walk that takes visitors along a series of narrow walkways, bridges, and tunnels that hug the rugged coastline. The entire walk is approximately 3 miles (4.8 kilometers) in length, with about 2 miles (3.2 kilometers) of the path being accessible to the public. The walk is physically demanding and requires a reasonable level of fitness, as it includes steep steps, uneven surfaces, and narrow passages.

The path begins at the Gobbins Visitor Centre, where visitors receive an introduction to the history and geology of the area. From there, a shuttle bus takes visitors to the starting point of the walk at Wise's Eye, a natural rock archway that marks the entrance to the cliff path.

Highlights of the Walk

The Tubular Bridge: One of the most iconic features of the Gobbins Cliff Path is the Tubular Bridge, a metal structure that curves around the face of the cliffs, providing spectacular views of the crashing waves below. Walking across this bridge is a thrilling experience and a highlight of the tour.

The Clifftop Views: Throughout the walk, visitors are treated to stunning vistas of the Irish Sea, the rugged coastline, and the distant horizon. On clear days, it is possible to see as far as Scotland and the Isle of Man.

Marine and Birdlife: The Gobbins Cliff Path is a haven for wildlife enthusiasts. The cliffs are home to a variety of seabirds, including puffins, guillemots, and kittiwakes. The surrounding waters are rich in marine life, and it is not uncommon to spot seals, dolphins, and even basking sharks.

The Swing Bridge: Another exhilarating feature of the path is the Swing Bridge, a suspension bridge that sways gently as visitors cross. This bridge offers an up-close view of the cliffs and the swirling waters below.

The Smugglers' Cave: The path also includes a tunnel known as the Smugglers' Cave, which adds an element of intrigue and history to the walk. This tunnel was historically used by smugglers to hide their contraband and offers a fascinating glimpse into the past.

The Amphitheatre: One of the most breathtaking sections of the walk is the Amphitheatre, a natural bowl-shaped formation in the cliffs where visitors can stop and take in the dramatic scenery.

Safety and Accessibility

Safety is a top priority at the Gobbins Cliff Path. The path is equipped with handrails, safety barriers, and non-slip surfaces to ensure the well-being of visitors. Guided tours are led by experienced guides who provide information on the history, geology, and wildlife of the area while ensuring that all safety protocols are followed.

Due to the challenging nature of the walk, it is not suitable for very young children, people with mobility issues, or those with a fear of heights. Visitors are advised to wear sturdy walking shoes and weather-appropriate clothing, as the coastal weather can be unpredictable.

Visitor Information

Booking and Tours: Due to the popularity of the Gobbins Cliff Path, advance booking is recommended. Tours are conducted in small groups to ensure safety and provide a personalized experience. Tickets can be purchased through the Gobbins Visitor Centre or their official website.

Getting There: The Gobbins Cliff Path is located near the village of Islandmagee, approximately 20 miles (32 kilometers) from Belfast. The site is accessible by car, and there is ample parking available at the Visitor Centre. Public transportation options include buses and trains from Belfast to Larne, followed by a short taxi ride to the Gobbins.

Facilities: The Gobbins Visitor Centre offers a range of facilities, including a cafe, gift shop, restrooms, and informational displays. The centre provides a comfortable starting point for the adventure and an opportunity to learn more about the path's history and natural environment.

Conclusion

The Gobbins Cliff Path is a spectacular and unique attraction that showcases the natural beauty and historical richness of Northern Ireland's coastline. The thrilling walk along the cliffs, combined with stunning views and fascinating wildlife, makes it an unforgettable experience for visitors. Whether you are an adventure seeker, a nature enthusiast, or a history buff, the Gobbins Cliff Path offers a one-of-a-kind journey that captures the essence of the rugged Irish coast.

Giant's Causeway

The Giant's Causeway is one of Northern Ireland's most iconic natural landmarks, renowned for its unique geological formations, stunning coastal scenery, and rich folklore. Located on the north coast of County Antrim, this UNESCO World Heritage Site attracts visitors from around the world who come to marvel at its distinctive basalt columns and explore its fascinating history and legends.

Geological Background

The Giant's Causeway was formed around 60 million years ago during a period of intense volcanic activity. As lava from ancient volcanic eruptions cooled rapidly, it contracted and fractured, creating a vast expanse of hexagonal basalt columns. These columns are arranged in a stepping-stone pattern that leads from the cliffs into the sea, resembling a grand causeway built by giants.

There are approximately 40,000 interlocking basalt columns at the Giant's Causeway, with the majority having six sides, though some have fewer or more sides. The columns vary in height, with the tallest reaching up to 12 meters (39 feet). This natural wonder is a testament to the powerful geological forces that shaped the Earth's surface millions of years ago.

Folklore and Legends

The Giant's Causeway is steeped in Irish mythology, with the most famous legend attributing its creation to the giant Finn McCool (Fionn mac Cumhaill). According to the legend, Finn McCool built the causeway to cross the sea and challenge his Scottish rival, Benandonner. When Finn realized that Benandonner was much larger and stronger, he devised a clever plan to avoid the fight.

Finn's wife, Oonagh, disguised Finn as a baby and tucked him into a cradle. When Benandonner saw the "baby," he assumed that Finn must be enormous if his child was so large. Frightened by this thought, Benandonner fled back to Scotland, destroying the causeway behind him to prevent Finn from following. This tale adds a layer of enchantment and intrigue to the already mesmerizing landscape.

Visiting the Giant's Causeway

The Giant's Causeway is managed by the National Trust, which provides facilities and services to enhance the visitor experience. The site is open year-round, and there are several ways to explore and enjoy this natural wonder.

Visitor Centre: The state-of-the-art Giant's Causeway Visitor Centre offers interactive exhibits, audio-visual displays, and informative panels that explain the geological history, wildlife, and mythology of the site. The centre also includes a cafe, gift shop, and restrooms.

Walking Trails: There are several walking trails of varying difficulty that allow visitors to explore the Giant's Causeway and the surrounding coastal landscape. The most popular route is the Blue Trail, a paved path that leads directly to the basalt columns. For more adventurous hikers, the Red Trail offers a longer and more challenging route along the cliff tops, providing breathtaking views of the coastline.

Guided Tours: Guided tours are available and highly recommended for those who want to gain deeper insights into the history, geology, and folklore of the Giant's Causeway. Knowledgeable guides share fascinating stories and scientific explanations, enriching the overall experience.

Causeway Coast: The Giant's Causeway is part of the larger Causeway Coast, a scenic stretch of coastline that includes other notable attractions such as Carrick-a-Rede Rope Bridge, Dunluce Castle, and the Carrickfergus Castle. Exploring the entire Causeway Coast offers a comprehensive experience of Northern Ireland's natural beauty and historical significance.

Wildlife and Nature: The area around the Giant's Causeway is rich in biodiversity, with a variety of bird species, marine life, and unique plant communities. Birdwatchers can spot species such as fulmars, razorbills, and guillemots, while the rock pools and coastal waters are home to crabs, starfish, and other marine creatures.

Tips for Visitors

Weather: The weather at the Giant's Causeway can be unpredictable, with strong winds and sudden changes in temperature. Visitors should dress in layers and wear sturdy, comfortable footwear suitable for walking on uneven surfaces.

Safety: While exploring the basalt columns and coastal trails, visitors should exercise caution and be aware of slippery surfaces, particularly when wet. It is important to stay within designated paths and follow safety guidelines provided by the National Trust.

Accessibility: The Visitor Centre and the Blue Trail are accessible to visitors with mobility challenges. There are also shuttle buses available from the Visitor Centre to the main causeway for those who may have difficulty walking the distance.

Conclusion

The Giant's Causeway is a natural wonder that captivates visitors with its extraordinary geological formations, breathtaking coastal views, and rich cultural heritage. Whether you are drawn by the scientific marvel of its basalt columns or the enchanting legends of Finn McCool, the Giant's Causeway offers an unforgettable experience. Its combination of natural beauty, historical significance, and mythological intrigue makes it a must-visit destination for anyone exploring Northern Ireland.

Carrickfergus Castle

Carrickfergus Castle is one of Northern Ireland's most impressive and well-preserved medieval structures, standing as a testament to the region's rich history and strategic importance. Located on the northern shore of Belfast Lough in the town of Carrickfergus, this imposing fortress has played a crucial role in the military, political, and social history of the area for over 800 years.

Historical Background

Carrickfergus Castle was built by John de Courcy, an Anglo-Norman knight who invaded Ulster in 1177. Recognizing the strategic significance of the site, de Courcy began constructing the castle in 1177 to establish his control over the region. The castle was initially a simple enclosure with wooden palisades but was soon developed into a formidable stone fortress.

Over the centuries, Carrickfergus Castle has seen numerous sieges and battles, changing hands between various factions, including the Normans, Scots, Irish, and English. It served as a military stronghold, a prison, and an armory, reflecting the turbulent history of the region. The castle was also a focal point during key historical events, such as the arrival of King William III in 1690 before the Battle of the Boyne.

Architectural Features

Carrickfergus Castle is notable for its robust and well-preserved architecture, which provides insight into medieval military engineering. Key features of the castle include:

The Keep: The central keep is the most prominent feature of Carrickfergus Castle. This large, rectangular tower was the primary residence and defensive stronghold. It has thick stone walls, narrow windows for archers, and a series of floors connected by spiral staircases.

The Outer Ward: Surrounding the keep is the outer ward, which includes additional defensive structures such as walls, towers, and a gatehouse. The outer walls are fortified with arrow slits and battlements, allowing defenders to protect the castle from invaders.

The Inner Ward: Within the outer ward is the inner ward, a more protected area that housed important buildings such as the great hall, chapel, and storage rooms. This area was the heart of the castle's domestic and administrative activities.

The Portcullis and Drawbridge: The castle's entrance was heavily fortified with a portcullis (a heavy iron gate) and a drawbridge that could be raised to prevent access. These features exemplify the defensive capabilities of the castle.

The Sea Gate: Carrickfergus Castle's position on the coast allowed for direct access to the sea. The sea gate enabled supplies and reinforcements to be delivered by boat, making the castle a vital link in regional trade and military logistics.

Visiting Carrickfergus Castle

Today, Carrickfergus Castle is managed by Northern Ireland Environment Agency and is open to the public. Visitors can explore the castle's well-preserved rooms, towers, and ramparts, gaining a sense of medieval life and the castle's strategic importance.

Exhibitions and Displays: The castle features a range of exhibits that showcase its history and significance. These include displays of medieval weapons and armor, as well as informative panels detailing the castle's construction, military history, and key events.

Guided Tours: Guided tours are available, providing visitors with detailed insights into the history, architecture, and stories of Carrickfergus Castle. Knowledgeable guides bring the history to life with anecdotes and explanations, enhancing the visitor experience.

Reenactments and Events: Throughout the year, Carrickfergus Castle hosts a variety of historical reenactments, festivals, and events. These include medieval fairs, battle reenactments, and educational programs that provide an immersive experience of medieval life and warfare.

Educational Programs: The castle offers educational programs for schools and groups, focusing on medieval history, archaeology, and the castle's role in regional history. These programs are designed to be engaging and informative, helping to foster a deeper understanding of the past.

Scenic Views: The castle's location on the shore of Belfast Lough provides stunning views of the water and the surrounding landscape. Visitors can walk along the battlements and enjoy panoramic views of the lough, the town of Carrickfergus, and the distant hills.

Practical Information

Opening Hours: Carrickfergus Castle is open to the public year-round, with seasonal variations in opening hours. It is advisable to check the official website or contact the castle directly for the most up-to-date information on opening times and ticket prices.

Accessibility: While some areas of the castle may present challenges for visitors with mobility issues due to narrow staircases and uneven surfaces, efforts have been made to improve accessibility. The visitor center and certain parts of the castle grounds are accessible to wheelchairs.

Facilities: The castle features a visitor center with restrooms, a gift shop, and informational displays. Nearby, the town of Carrickfergus offers a range of amenities, including cafes, restaurants, and shops.

Location and Transport: Carrickfergus Castle is easily accessible by car, bus, and train. It is located approximately 11 miles (18 kilometers) from Belfast, making it a convenient day trip from the city. Ample parking is available near the castle.

Conclusion

Carrickfergus Castle stands as a remarkable monument to Northern Ireland's medieval past, offering a rich blend of history, architecture, and scenic beauty. Its well-preserved structures and informative exhibits provide a fascinating glimpse into the life and times of those who lived and fought within its walls. Whether you are a history enthusiast, a family looking for an educational outing, or a traveler seeking to explore Northern Ireland's cultural heritage, Carrickfergus Castle is a must-visit destination that promises a memorable and enriching experience.

Chapter 6: Practical Information

Accommodation

Belfast offers a wide range of accommodation options to suit all tastes and budgets, from luxury hotels and boutique guesthouses to budget-friendly hostels and self-catering apartments. Whether you are visiting for business, leisure, or a bit of both, you can find the perfect place to stay that meets your needs and preferences. Here is a guide to some of the best accommodation options in Belfast.

Luxury Hotels

The Fitzwilliam Hotel

Location: Great Victoria Street, City Center

The Fitzwilliam Hotel is a five-star luxury hotel located in the heart of Belfast, adjacent to the Grand Opera House. This stylish and contemporary hotel offers elegantly designed rooms and suites, a fine-dining restaurant, a chic bar, and a well-equipped fitness center. The Fitzwilliam Hotel is known for its exceptional service and attention to detail, making it a top choice for travellers seeking luxury and comfort.

The Merchant Hotel

Location: Skipper Street, Cathedral Quarter

Housed in a grand Victorian building that was once the headquarters of the Ulster Bank, The Merchant Hotel is a five-star establishment that combines historic charm with modern luxury. The hotel features opulent rooms and suites, a rooftop gym and spa, a jazz bar, and the renowned Great Room Restaurant. The Merchant Hotel is an excellent choice for those looking to indulge in a lavish and memorable stay.

Boutique Hotels and Guesthouses

Tara Lodge

Location: Cromwell Road, Queen's Quarter

Tara Lodge is a boutique guesthouse offering stylish and comfortable accommodation in the Queen's Quarter, close to Queen's University and Botanic Gardens. The guesthouse features modern rooms with luxurious bedding, flat-screen TVs, and complimentary Wi-Fi. A full breakfast is included, and the friendly staff are always on hand to provide recommendations and assistance. Tara Lodge is perfect for travelers seeking a personalized and cozy experience.

The Harrison Chambers of Distinction

Location: Malone Road, Queen's Quarter

The Harrison Chambers of Distinction is a beautifully restored Victorian townhouse that offers a unique and elegant accommodation experience. Each room is individually decorated with antique furnishings and modern amenities, creating a blend of old-world charm and contemporary comfort. The guesthouse is located near Queen's University and is within walking distance of many attractions, making it an ideal base for exploring the city.

Bullitt Hotel

Location: Church Lane, City Center

Bullitt Hotel is a trendy and modern boutique hotel in the heart of Belfast's city center. The hotel features stylish rooms with minimalist design, a rooftop bar with stunning views, and an on-site restaurant offering delicious and creative dishes. Bullitt Hotel is known for its vibrant atmosphere and is a great choice for young travelers and those looking for a lively and contemporary stay.

Mid-Range Hotels

AC Hotel by Marriott Belfast

Location: Donegall Quay, City Center

Located along the River Lagan, the AC Hotel by Marriott Belfast offers comfortable and modern accommodation with beautiful waterfront views. The hotel features well-appointed rooms, a fitness center, and an on-site restaurant serving European-inspired cuisine. Its central location makes it convenient for exploring the city's attractions, shopping, and dining options.

Holiday Inn Belfast City Centre

Location: Hope Street, City Center

The Holiday Inn Belfast City Centre provides comfortable and affordable accommodation in a convenient location, close to Great Victoria Street Station and the city's main attractions. The hotel features modern rooms with amenities such as free Wi-Fi, flat-screen TVs, and a fitness center. An on-site restaurant and bar offer a range of dining options, making it a great choice for both business and leisure travelers.

Maldron Hotel Belfast City

Location: Brunswick Street, City Center

The Maldron Hotel Belfast City offers contemporary accommodation in the heart of the city, within walking distance of major landmarks such as City Hall and the Grand Opera House. The hotel features spacious rooms with modern amenities, an on-site restaurant and bar, and meeting facilities for business travelers. Its central location and comfortable accommodations make it a popular choice for visitors.

Budget-Friendly Options

Vagabonds Hostel

Location: University Road, Queen's Quarter

Vagabonds Hostel is a popular and highly-rated hostel located near Queen's University. The hostel offers a range of dormitory and private rooms, along with communal areas, a fully equipped kitchen, and a lively social atmosphere. Vagabonds is known for its friendly staff, cleanliness, and affordability, making it a top choice for budget-conscious travelers and backpackers.

Belfast International Youth Hostel

Location: Donegall Road, City Center

The Belfast International Youth Hostel provides budget-friendly accommodation in a central location, just a short walk from the city center and major attractions. The hostel offers a variety of room types, from dormitories to private en-suite rooms, as well as communal areas, a self-catering kitchen, and an on-site cafe. It is a great option for travelers looking for affordable accommodation with convenient access to the city's highlights.

ETAP Hotel Belfast

Location: Dublin Road, City Center

The ETAP Hotel Belfast offers clean and basic accommodation at an affordable price. The hotel features compact rooms with modern amenities, free Wi-Fi, and a 24-hour reception. Its central location, close to the city's entertainment district and main attractions, makes it a convenient choice for budget travelers.

Self-Catering Apartments

Dream Apartments Belfast

Location: Obel Tower and St. Thomas Hall, City Center

Dream Apartments Belfast offers a range of serviced apartments that provide the comfort and convenience of home with the amenities of a hotel. The apartments are fully furnished and include modern kitchens, spacious living areas, and free Wi-Fi. Their central locations in the Obel Tower and St. Thomas Hall make them ideal for extended stays and families seeking flexible accommodation options.

Central Belfast Apartments

Location: Various locations, City Center

Central Belfast Apartments offers a selection of self-catering apartments in prime locations throughout the city center. Each apartment is well-equipped with modern conveniences, including full kitchens, laundry facilities, and free Wi-Fi. These apartments provide a comfortable and flexible accommodation option for travelers looking for a home-away-from-home experience.

Conclusion

Belfast offers a diverse range of accommodation options to suit every traveler's needs and budget. From luxurious five-star hotels and charming boutique guesthouses to budget-friendly hostels and convenient self-catering apartments, the city provides a variety of choices for a comfortable and enjoyable stay. Whether you're visiting for business, leisure, or a mix of both, you're sure to find the perfect place to stay in Belfast.

Transportation

Transportation in Belfast

Belfast offers a comprehensive transportation network that makes it easy for residents and visitors to navigate the city and its surrounding areas. Whether you prefer public transit, cycling, walking, or driving, Belfast has a variety of options to suit your travel needs. Here's a guide to the different modes of transportation available in Belfast.

Public Transport

Translink

Translink is the main public transportation provider in Belfast, operating the Metro, Glider, Ulsterbus, and NI Railways services. Translink offers a range of ticketing options, including single fares, day tickets, and weekly or monthly passes.

Metro Buses

The Metro bus service is the primary mode of public transport within Belfast. The network consists of 12 corridors, each with multiple routes that cover the city and its suburbs. Metro buses are frequent and provide convenient access to major attractions, shopping areas, and residential neighborhoods. The buses are modern, accessible, and equipped with free Wi-Fi.

Glider Buses

The Glider is a rapid transit bus service that operates on two main routes: G1 (East to West Belfast) and G2 (Titanic Quarter to City Centre). The Glider buses feature modern design, dedicated lanes, and priority at traffic signals, ensuring a quick and efficient journey. The Glider service is a popular choice for commuters and tourists alike, offering a smooth and reliable way to travel across the city.

Ulsterbus

Ulsterbus provides regional bus services connecting Belfast with other towns and cities in Northern Ireland. These buses are ideal for day trips and excursions outside the city, offering comfortable and convenient travel to destinations such as the Giant's Causeway, Derry/Londonderry, and more.

NI Railways

NI Railways operates train services that connect Belfast with various destinations across Northern Ireland and beyond. The main railway stations in Belfast are Lanyon Place (formerly Belfast Central), Great Victoria Street, and Botanic. The train network provides efficient connections to cities such as Bangor, Newry, Portrush, and Derry/Londonderry. Trains are comfortable, with amenities such as free Wi-Fi and catering services on some routes.

Taxis and Ride-Sharing

Taxis

Taxis are readily available throughout Belfast, with several companies offering reliable services. Black taxis can be hailed on the street, found at taxi ranks, or booked by phone or app. Private hire taxis must be booked in advance. Taxis are a convenient option for quick and direct travel, especially for airport transfers or late-night journeys.

Ride-Sharing

Ride-sharing services like Uber are available in Belfast, providing an alternative to traditional taxis. These services can be booked via mobile apps, offering a convenient and often cost-effective way to get around the city.

Cycling

Belfast is becoming increasingly cycle-friendly, with dedicated bike lanes, cycling routes, and bike-sharing schemes making it easier to explore the city on two wheels.

Belfast Bikes

Just Eat Belfast Bikes is a public bike-sharing scheme with numerous docking stations located around the city. Bikes can be rented for short journeys, with affordable pricing options for casual users and subscribers. This service is ideal for tourists and locals looking for a quick and eco-friendly way to get around.

Cycling Routes

Belfast boasts several scenic cycling routes, including the Comber Greenway, Lagan Towpath, and the routes around the Titanic Quarter. These routes offer safe and enjoyable cycling experiences, connecting key areas of the city and providing access to beautiful natural landscapes.

Walking

Belfast is a compact and walkable city, with many attractions, shopping areas, and dining options located within easy walking distance. The city center is particularly pedestrian-friendly, with wide sidewalks, pedestrianized zones, and well-marked crossings.

Walking Tours

For those interested in exploring the city on foot, there are numerous walking tours available that cover various themes such as history, architecture, street art, and food. Guided tours provide valuable insights and enhance the overall experience of discovering Belfast.

Car Hire and Driving

Car Hire

Several car rental companies operate in Belfast, with offices located at the airports, city center, and other convenient locations. Hiring a car provides flexibility and freedom to explore Belfast and the surrounding countryside at your own pace. It's particularly useful for visiting attractions outside the city, such as the Giant's Causeway, Mourne Mountains, and the Antrim Coast.

Driving in Belfast

Driving in Belfast is relatively straightforward, with well-maintained roads and clear signage. However, traffic can be heavy during peak hours, and parking in the city center can be challenging. There are several public car parks and on-street parking options available, but it's advisable to check parking regulations and fees.

Air Travel

George Best Belfast City Airport (BHD)

Located just a few miles from the city center, George Best Belfast City Airport primarily serves domestic flights and short-haul international routes. It's easily accessible by car, taxi, and public transport, making it a convenient option for travelers.

Belfast International Airport (BFS)

Situated about 13 miles northwest of Belfast, Belfast International Airport is the city's main airport, offering a wide range of domestic and international flights. The airport is accessible by car, taxi, and the Airport

Express 300 bus service, which provides regular connections to the city center.

Ferry Services

Belfast is well-connected by ferry to other parts of the UK and Ireland. Stena Line operates ferry services from Belfast to Cairnryan in Scotland and Liverpool in England. These services are ideal for travelers bringing their own vehicles or those who prefer a scenic sea journey.

Conclusion

Belfast's comprehensive transportation network ensures that getting around the city and its surroundings is convenient and efficient. Whether you prefer public transport, cycling, walking, or driving, there are plenty of options to suit your needs. With its well-connected infrastructure and range of travel choices, exploring Belfast and its beautiful landscapes is both easy and enjoyable.

Safety Tips

Safety Tips for Visitors to Belfast

Belfast is a vibrant and welcoming city, but like any urban area, it's important to stay mindful of safety. By following some basic safety tips, you can ensure a pleasant and secure visit. Here are some guidelines to help you stay safe while exploring Belfast.

General Safety Tips

Stay Aware of Your Surroundings
- Be aware of your surroundings at all times, especially in crowded areas or unfamiliar neighborhoods.
- Keep an eye on your belongings and avoid displaying valuable items like expensive jewelry or electronics.

Emergency Numbers
- In case of emergencies, dial 999 or 112 to reach emergency services (police, fire, ambulance).
- For non-emergency situations requiring police assistance, dial 101.

Local Laws and Customs
- Respect local laws and customs, and be mindful of cultural sensitivities.

- Avoid discussing sensitive political topics, as Northern Ireland has a complex history of political and sectarian tensions.

Personal Safety

Walking Around
- Stick to well-lit and populated areas, especially at night.
- If possible, travel with a companion or in groups after dark.
- Avoid shortcuts through alleys, parks, or unlit areas.
- Using Public Transport
- Use official public transport services like Metro buses, Glider, and NI Railways.
- Keep an eye on your belongings and be cautious of pickpockets, especially in crowded buses and trains.
- Taxis and Ride-Sharing
- Use licensed taxis or reputable ride-sharing services like Uber.
- If using a taxi, check for a proper taxi license and identification.
- Avoid accepting rides from unlicensed or unmarked vehicles.

Accommodation Safety

Hotel and Hostel Safety
- Choose reputable accommodation with good reviews and safety features.

- Keep your room locked and use the room safe to store valuables.
- Familiarize yourself with emergency exits and procedures.
- Apartment Rentals
- If renting an apartment, ensure it's from a reputable source such as Airbnb or a licensed rental agency.
- Verify the security of the property, including locks, alarms, and neighborhood safety.

Health and Wellbeing

- Medical Assistance
- Know the location of the nearest hospital or medical facility.
- Carry essential medications and a basic first aid kit.
- Purchase travel insurance that covers medical expenses and emergencies.
- Covid-19 Precautions
- Follow local Covid-19 guidelines, which may include wearing masks, practicing social distancing, and using hand sanitizer.
- Stay informed about any travel restrictions or requirements before your visit.

Financial Safety

- ATM and Card Safety
- Use ATMs located in well-lit, busy areas or inside banks.

- Cover the keypad when entering your PIN and be cautious of anyone standing too close.
- Notify your bank of your travel plans to avoid issues with your credit or debit cards.
- Cash and Valuables
- Carry only the cash you need for the day and keep the rest secured in your accommodation.
- Avoid flashing large amounts of cash in public.

Road Safety

- Driving in Belfast
- Drive on the left side of the road and familiarize yourself with local traffic laws.
- Always wear seatbelts and avoid using mobile phones while driving.
- Be cautious of pedestrians and cyclists, especially in busy city areas.
- Cycling and Walking
- Use designated cycling lanes and pedestrian paths where available.
- Wear a helmet when cycling and use lights and reflectors for visibility.
- Cross streets at designated pedestrian crossings and obey traffic signals.
- Social and Nightlife Safety

Nightlife Precautions
- Stick to well-known and reputable bars, clubs, and restaurants.
- Avoid accepting drinks from strangers and keep an eye on your drink to prevent spiking.

- Plan your journey home in advance and use licensed taxis or ride-sharing services.

Meeting New People
- Be cautious when meeting new people and avoid sharing personal information too quickly.
- Arrange to meet in public places and inform a friend or family member of your plans.
- Outdoor and Adventure Safety

Outdoor Activities
- If hiking or exploring outdoor areas, inform someone of your plans and expected return time.
- Carry a map, compass, and sufficient supplies, including water, food, and appropriate clothing.
- Stay on marked trails and avoid risky behaviors like cliff diving or venturing into unmarked areas.
- Weather Conditions
- Check the weather forecast before heading out and be prepared for sudden changes.
- Dress in layers and carry rain gear, as Belfast's weather can be unpredictable.

Emergency Contacts and Information

- Keep a list of emergency contacts, including local authorities, your country's embassy or consulate, and family members.
- Know the location and contact information of your accommodation.

Conclusion

Belfast is a safe and welcoming city with a lot to offer visitors. By following these safety tips and staying aware of your surroundings, you can ensure a pleasant and secure visit. Enjoy your time exploring Belfast's rich history, vibrant culture, and beautiful landscapes while keeping these guidelines in mind.

Local Customs and Etiquette

Local Customs and Etiquette in Belfast

Belfast is a vibrant city with a rich cultural heritage and a welcoming atmosphere. To ensure a pleasant and respectful visit, it's helpful to familiarize yourself with local customs and etiquette. Here are some guidelines to help you navigate social interactions and cultural norms in Belfast.

Greeting and Social Interaction

Greetings
- A friendly handshake is a common way to greet someone in Belfast, especially when meeting for the first time.
- It's polite to smile and make eye contact during greetings.
- In informal settings, people often greet each other with a friendly "hello" or "hi."

Titles and Formality

Use titles (Mr., Mrs., Miss, Dr.) and last names when addressing someone you've just met or in formal situations.

First names are commonly used once you become more familiar with someone.

It's respectful to ask how someone prefers to be addressed.

Politeness and Courtesy

Northern Irish people are generally polite and appreciate good manners. Saying "please," "thank you," and "excuse me" is important.

Holding doors open for others and offering seats to elderly or disabled individuals is considered courteous.

Apologizing if you accidentally bump into someone is expected.

Dining Etiquette

Invitations

If you're invited to someone's home for a meal, it's customary to bring a small gift, such as a bottle of wine, flowers, or chocolates.

Punctuality is appreciated, so try to arrive on time.

Table Manners

Wait for the host to indicate where you should sit.

Keep your hands on the table, but not your elbows.

Begin eating only after everyone has been served and the host starts eating.

Use utensils for most foods, and follow the lead of your host or others if you're unsure.

In Restaurants

It's customary to wait to be seated by a host or server.

Tipping is appreciated but not obligatory. A tip of 10-15% is standard if you received good service.

When paying the bill, you can ask for separate checks if you are dining with a group, but it's polite to mention this when you order.

Public Behavior

Queuing

Northern Irish people are very orderly about queuing (standing in line). Always take your place at the end of the line and wait your turn.

Cutting in line is considered very rude.

Public Transportation

Offer your seat to elderly, disabled, or pregnant individuals.

Avoid talking loudly on public transportation or playing music without headphones.

Have your ticket or fare ready before boarding to avoid holding up the line.

Littering

Keep Belfast clean by disposing of litter properly in bins provided throughout the city.
Recycling bins are often available for sorting different types of waste.

Cultural Sensitivity

Political and Historical Sensitivity

Northern Ireland has a complex political history. It's best to avoid discussing politics, religion, or the Troubles (the period of conflict from the late 1960s to 1998) unless you are very familiar with your conversation partners and know they are comfortable with such topics.

Respect the different symbols and emblems associated with unionist and nationalist communities.

Local Pride

Belfast residents are proud of their city and its heritage. Show interest and appreciation for local customs, traditions, and landmarks.

Attending local events, festivals, and markets is a great way to engage with the culture.

Dress Code

General Attire

Casual attire is common for everyday activities. Jeans, t-shirts, and comfortable shoes are widely accepted.

For dining out, smart casual attire is usually appropriate unless otherwise specified.

Formal Occasions

For formal events, such as weddings or business meetings, dressing more formally is expected. Men might wear suits and ties, and women might wear dresses or business attire.

Weather Considerations

Belfast weather can be unpredictable. It's advisable to carry an umbrella and wear layers to adjust to changing conditions.

Language

English

English is the primary language spoken in Belfast. Most locals have a distinct Northern Irish accent, which can vary across regions. If you don't understand something, politely ask the person to repeat it.

Irish (Gaeilge)

While Irish (Gaeilge) is not widely spoken in Belfast, some signs and place names are bilingual. Showing interest in the Irish language can be appreciated depending where you are in Belfast.

Local Slang

Belfast has its own local slang and expressions. Don't be afraid to ask for clarification if you hear something unfamiliar.

Respect for Local Businesses

Shopping and Dining Local
Supporting local businesses, shops, and restaurants is appreciated and helps sustain the local economy.
Many businesses may have specific opening hours, so it's good to check in advance.

Payment
Credit and debit cards are widely accepted, but it's always good to have some cash on hand for small purchases or in case of card machine issues.

Conclusion

By understanding and respecting the local customs and etiquette in Belfast, you can ensure a positive and respectful interaction with the people and culture of the city. Enjoy your visit to Belfast by embracing its rich heritage, friendly atmosphere, and vibrant community while keeping these guidelines in mind.

Useful Contacts

Useful Contacts for Visitors to Belfast

Having a list of useful contacts can greatly enhance your experience and ensure that you are prepared for any situation that may arise during your visit to Belfast. Below is a compilation of important contact information for emergency services, transportation, tourism, and more.

Emergency Services

- Emergency Services (Police, Fire, Ambulance)
    - Phone: 999 or 112

- Non-Emergency Police
    - Phone: 101

- Medical Services

- Belfast City Hospital
    - Address: 51 Lisburn Road, Belfast BT9 7AB
    - Phone: +44 28 9032 9241

- Royal Victoria Hospital
    - Address: 274 Grosvenor Road, Belfast BT12 6BA
    - Phone: +44 28 9024 0503

- Mater Infirmorum Hospital

- Address: 45-51 Crumlin Road, Belfast BT14 6AB
- Phone: +44 28 9074 1211

- NHS 24/7 Health Advice
    - Phone: 111

- Travel and Transportation

- Translink (Public Transport Information)
    - Phone: +44 28 9066 6630
    - Website: [Translink](https://www.translink.co.uk)

- George Best Belfast City Airport
    - Address: Belfast BT3 9JH
    - Phone: +44 28 9093 9093
    - Website: [Belfast City Airport](https://www.belfastcityairport.com)

- Belfast International Airport
    - Address: Belfast BT29 4AB
    - Phone: +44 28 9448 4848
    - Website: [Belfast International Airport](https://www.belfastairport.com)

- Taxi Services
    - Value Cabs
    - Phone: +44 28 9080 9080
    - Website: [Value Cabs](https://www.valuecabs.co.uk)

- FonaCab
- Phone: +44 28 9033 3333
- Website: [FonaCab](https://www.fonacab.com)

- Tourist Information

- Visit Belfast Welcome Centre
  - Address: 9 Donegall Square North, Belfast BT1 5GB
  - Phone: +44 28 9024 6609
  - Website: [Visit Belfast](https://visitbelfast.com)

- Northern Ireland Tourist Board
  - Phone: +44 28 9023 1221
  - Website: [Discover Northern Ireland](https://discovernorthernireland.com)

- Embassies and Consulates

- United States Consulate
  - Address: Danesfort House, 223 Stranmillis Road, Belfast BT9 5GR
  - Phone: +44 28 9038 6100
  - Website: [U.S. Consulate Belfast](https://uk.usembassy.gov/embassy-consulates/belfast)

- Canadian Consulate (Honorary)

- Address: Scottish Provident Building, 7 Donegall Square W, Belfast BT1 6JH
- Phone: +44 28 9024 4164

- Australian Consulate (Honorary)
    - Address: 83 Victoria Street, Belfast BT1 4PB
    - Phone: +44 28 9023 6040

- Financial Services

- Currency Exchange
    - Travelex at Belfast International Airport
    - Phone: +44 28 9445 2848
    - Website: [Travelex](https://www.travelex.co.uk)

- Major Banks
    - Bank of Ireland
    - Phone: +44 28 9043 3000
    - Website: [Bank of Ireland](https://www.bankofirelanduk.com)

    - Ulster Bank
    - Phone: +44 28 9035 7957
    - Website: [Ulster Bank](https://www.ulsterbank.co.uk)

    - Danske Bank
    - Phone: +44 28 9004 5500
    - Website: [Danske Bank](https://www.danskebank.co.uk)

- Communication

- Main Post Office
    - Address: 12-16 Bridge Street, Belfast BT1 1LT
    - Phone: +44 28 9023 3401
    - Website: [Post Office](https://www.postoffice.co.uk)

- Utility Services

- Electricity (Northern Ireland Electricity - NIE)
    - Emergency Phone: 03457 643 643
    - Website: [NIE Networks](https://www.nienetworks.co.uk)

- Water (Northern Ireland Water)
    - Emergency Phone: 03457 440 088
    - Website: [NI Water](https://www.niwater.com)

- Additional Contacts

- Citizens Advice Bureau
    - Phone: +44 28 9023 1120
    - Website: [Citizens Advice](https://www.citizensadvice.org.uk/nireland)

- Belfast City Council
    - Phone: +44 28 9032 0202

- Website: [Belfast City Council](https://www.belfastcity.gov.uk)

Having these contacts handy can help ensure that your stay in Belfast is safe, convenient, and enjoyable. Whether you need assistance in an emergency, information on local attractions, or help navigating the city, these resources are available to support you.

Appendices

Maps

- Belfast City Center Map

    - Provides a detailed overview of the main streets, attractions, and key points of interest in the city center.
    - Available at the Visit Belfast Welcome Centre or downloadable from the [Visit Belfast website](https://visitbelfast.com/).

- Belfast Public Transport Map

    - Displays bus and Glider routes, as well as train lines within the city and surrounding areas.
    - Available from Translink offices or downloadable from the [Translink website](https://www.translink.co.uk/).

- Belfast Walking and Cycling Maps

    - Highlights walking and cycling routes, including scenic trails and paths like the Lagan Towpath and the Comber Greenway.
    - Available at local bike shops, tourist information centers, or downloadable from the [Belfast City Council

website](https://www.belfastcity.gov.uk).

- Key Attraction Maps

- Giant's Causeway Map

    - Provides detailed information on the walking trails, visitor facilities, and points of interest at the Giant's Causeway.
    - Available at the Giant's Causeway Visitor Centre or downloadable from the [National Trust website](https://www.nationaltrust.org.uk/giants-causeway).

- Carrickfergus Castle Map

    - Offers an overview of the castle grounds, visitor facilities, and key historical points.
    - Available at Carrickfergus Castle or downloadable from the [Northern Ireland Environment Agency website](https://www.nidirect.gov.uk).

- Accommodation and Dining Maps

- Hotel Locations Map

    - Shows the locations of major hotels and accommodation options in Belfast.

- Available at the Visit Belfast Welcome Centre or downloadable from the [Visit Belfast website](https://visitbelfast.com/).

- Restaurant and Pub Guide Map

    - Highlights popular dining and nightlife spots throughout the city.
    - Available at tourist information centers or downloadable from the [Visit Belfast website](https://visitbelfast.com/).

- Emergency and Services Maps

- Emergency Services Map

    - Provides the locations of hospitals, police stations, and fire stations in Belfast.
    - Available at the Visit Belfast Welcome Centre or downloadable from the [Belfast City Council website](https://www.belfastcity.gov.uk).

- Downloadable and Interactive Maps

- Google Maps

    - Offers detailed and interactive maps with navigation features for driving,

walking, cycling, and public transportation.
- Accessible via the [Google Maps website](https://maps.google.com) or mobile app.

- Citymapper

    - Provides detailed public transport maps and real-time navigation within Belfast.
    - Accessible via the [Citymapper website](https://citymapper.com/belfast) or mobile app.

- OpenStreetMap

    - A detailed and editable map of Belfast and its surroundings, created by a community of mappers.
    - Accessible via the [OpenStreetMap website](https://www.openstreetmap.org).

- Tourist Information Centers

- Visit Belfast Welcome Centre

    - Location: 9 Donegall Square North, Belfast BT1 5GB
    - Phone: +44 28 9024 6609
    - Website: [Visit Belfast](https://visitbelfast.com)

- The Visit Belfast Welcome Centre offers a wide range of maps, guides, and brochures to help you navigate the city and plan your visit. Staff at the center can also provide personalized recommendations and assistance.

- By utilizing these maps and resources, you can easily explore Belfast, find key attractions, navigate public transportation, and discover the best places to eat and stay. Enjoy your visit to this vibrant and historic city!

Index

- A
  - Accommodation
  - Luxury Hotels: The Fitzwilliam Hotel, The Merchant Hotel
  - Boutique Hotels and Guesthouses: Tara Lodge, The Harrison Chambers of Distinction, Bullitt Hotel
  - Mid-Range Hotels: AC Hotel by Marriott Belfast, Holiday Inn Belfast City Centre, Maldron Hotel Belfast City
  - Budget-Friendly Options: Vagabonds Hostel, Belfast International Youth Hostel, ETAP Hotel Belfast
  - Self-Catering Apartments: Dream Apartments Belfast, Central Belfast Apartments

  - Airports
  - George Best Belfast City Airport
  - Belfast International Airport

- B
  - Belfast Castle
  - Historical Background
  - Architectural Features
  - Gardens and Grounds
  - Events and Activities
  - Visitor Information

  - Belfast Zoo
  - Historical Background
  - Animal Collection
  - Conservation and Research
  - Education and Outreach
  - Visitor Experience

- C
  - Carrickfergus Castle
  - Historical Background
  - Architectural Features
  - Visiting Carrickfergus Castle
  - Practical Information

  - Cave Hill
  - Geological and Natural Features
  - Historical Significance
  - Outdoor Activities
  - Folklore and Legends
  - Conservation and Community

  - City Maps
  - Belfast City Center Map
  - Belfast Public Transport Map
  - Belfast Walking and Cycling Maps

- E
  - Emergency Services
  - Emergency Numbers
  - Hospitals: Belfast City Hospital, Royal Victoria Hospital, Mater Infirmorum Hospital
  - NHS 24/7 Health Advice

  - Embassies and Consulates
  - United States Consulate
  - Canadian Consulate (Honorary)
  - Australian Consulate (Honorary)

- F
  - Financial Services
  - Currency Exchange: Travelex at Belfast International Airport
  - Major Banks: Bank of Ireland, Ulster Bank, Danske Bank

- G
    - Giant's Causeway
    - Geological Background
    - Folklore and Legends
    - Visiting the Giant's Causeway
    - Tips for Visitors

    - Gobbins Cliff Path
    - Historical Background
    - The Walk
    - Highlights of the Walk
    - Safety and Accessibility
    - Visitor Information

- H
    - Health and Wellbeing
    - Medical Assistance
    - Covid-19 Precautions

- L
    - Local Customs and Etiquette
    - Greeting and Social Interaction
    - Dining Etiquette
    - Public Behavior
    - Cultural Sensitivity
    - Dress Code
    - Language
    - Respect for Local Businesses

- M
    - Maps
    - City Maps
    - Key Attraction Maps
    - Accommodation and Dining Maps
    - Emergency and Services Maps
    - Downloadable and Interactive Maps
    - Tourist Information Centers

- O
  - Off-the-Beaten-Path Museums
  - The War Memorial Museum
  - The Museum of Orange Heritage
  - The Irish Republican History Museum
  - The Transport Museum
  - The Flame Gasworks Museum
  - The Linen Hall Library
  - The Royal Ulster Rifles Museum
  - The HMS Caroline

  - Outdoor and Adventure Safety
  - Outdoor Activities
  - Weather Conditions

- P
  - Personal Safety
  - Walking Around
  - Using Public Transport
  - Taxis and Ride-Sharing

- R
  - Road Safety
  - Driving in Belfast
  - Cycling and Walking

- S
  - Safety Tips
  - General Safety Tips
  - Personal Safety
  - Accommodation Safety
  - Health and Wellbeing
  - Financial Safety
  - Road Safety
  - Social and Nightlife Safety
  - Outdoor and Adventure Safety
  - Emergency Contacts and Information

- Social and Nightlife Safety
- Nightlife Precautions
- Meeting New People

- T
  - Transportation
  - Public Transport: Translink, Metro Buses, Glider Buses, Ulsterbus, NI Railways
  - Taxis and Ride-Sharing
  - Cycling: Belfast Bikes, Cycling Routes
  - Walking
  - Car Hire and Driving
  - Air Travel: George Best Belfast City Airport, Belfast International Airport
  - Ferry Services

  - Tourist Information
  - Visit Belfast Welcome Centre
  - Northern Ireland Tourist Board

  - Utility Services
  - Electricity (Northern Ireland Electricity - NIE)
  - Water (Northern Ireland Water)

This index provides a comprehensive guide to key topics and points of interest covered in this document, ensuring you can easily find the information you need for your visit to Belfast.

Acknowledgments

Acknowledgments

Creating this comprehensive guide to Belfast has been a collaborative effort, and we are grateful to all those who contributed their time, expertise, and insights to make this resource as informative and useful as possible. We would like to extend our heartfelt thanks to the following:

- Contributors and Researchers
    - Local Historians: For providing invaluable information on Belfast's rich history and heritage.
    - Tourism Experts: For sharing their knowledge of must-see attractions, hidden gems, and practical travel tips.
    - Conservationists and Wildlife Experts: For offering insights into the natural beauty and biodiversity of the region.
    - Cultural Organizations: For highlighting the vibrant arts, music, and cultural scene in Belfast.

- Local Businesses and Services
    - Hotels and Accommodation Providers: For sharing details about their services and amenities, ensuring visitors have a comfortable stay.

- Restaurants, Cafes, and Pubs: For recommending the best places to enjoy local cuisine and hospitality.
- Transportation Services: For providing essential information on navigating the city and beyond.

- Government and Tourism Boards
  - Visit Belfast: For their extensive resources and support in promoting Belfast as a tourist destination.
  - Northern Ireland Tourist Board: For their commitment to showcasing the beauty and culture of Northern Ireland.

- Community Members and Local Residents
  - Belfast Residents: For their warm hospitality and willingness to share their city with visitors.
  - Local Guides and Volunteers: For their dedication to enhancing the visitor experience through informative tours and community events.

- Creative and Technical Support
  - Photographers and Visual Artists: For capturing the essence of Belfast through stunning images and illustrations.
  - Writers and Editors: For their meticulous work in compiling, writing, and refining the content of this guide.
  - Designers and Layout Specialists: For creating an engaging and user-friendly format.

- Special Thanks
    - To all the visitors and travelers who continue to explore and appreciate the wonders of Belfast. Your enthusiasm and curiosity inspire us to keep sharing the beauty and history of this remarkable city.

- Personal Acknowledgments
    - To our families and friends for their unwavering support and encouragement throughout the creation of this guide.

This guide is a testament to the collaborative spirit and shared love for Belfast. We hope it serves as a valuable resource for all who seek to discover and enjoy the many facets of this vibrant city. Thank you to everyone who played a part in bringing this project to life.

Printed in Great Britain
by Amazon